The Art Of
BUSINESS
SOFTWARE

A Comprehensive Guide for Success

By
Danish Ali Bajwa & Usama Bajwa

Copyright © 2023 By Danish Ali Bajwa, Usama Bajwa,

The content contained within this book may not be reproduced, duplicated, or transmitted in any form or retrieval system now known or to be invented without direct written permission from the author or publisher. Under no circumstances will any blame or legal responsibility be held against the publisher, or author, for any damages, reparation, or monetary loss due to the information contained within this book. Either directly or indirectly.

Legal Notice:

This book is copyright protected. This book is only for personal use. You cannot amend, distribute, sell, use, quote, or paraphrase any part of the content within this book without the author or publisher's consent. "Fair Use" means a summary or quote with appropriate credit to the author is permitted.

Disclaimer Notice:

Please note the information contained within this book is for educational purposes only. All effort has been executed to present accurate, up-to-date, reliable, and complete information. No warranties of any kind are declared or implied. Readers acknowledge that the author is not rendering legal, financial, medical, or professional advice. The content within this book has been derived from various sources. Please consult a qualified professional before attempting any techniques outlined in this book. By reading and using this book, the reader agrees that under no circumstances is the author responsible for any direct or indirect losses incurred due to the use of the information within this book, including, but not limited to, — errors, omissions, or inaccuracies.

Email: rkbooks16@gmail.com

EBOOK ISBN: 978-969-3492-06-4

PAPERBACK ISBN: 978-969-3492-07-1

HARDBACK ISBN: 978-969-3492-08-8

Authors Bio

Danish Ali Bajwa and Usama Bajwa, collectively known as the Bajwa Brothers, are a dynamic writing duo known for their vast array of published works spanning several genres. Born and raised in a home where creativity and knowledge were deeply valued, these brothers harnessed their intrinsic knack for storytelling and exploration into a thriving career in literature.

Danish Ali Bajwa is a prolific writer with a unique ability to connect with a diverse audience. With a distinct voice, he has contributed to an extensive collection of children's books, where he elegantly interweaves essential life lessons with engaging narratives that resonate with young minds. Beyond children's literature, Usama's portfolio also includes a number of motivational books. He has an uncanny knack for uplifting and inspiring readers through his compelling narratives and authentic portrayals of the human spirit. Usama's words serve as a beacon of positivity, inspiring readers to conquer their fears and reach their true potential.

Usama Bajwa, on the other hand, brings an analytical perspective to their writing collaboration. With a keen interest in the intersection of business and technology, Danish has written several informative books, making complex topics accessible and engaging for readers. Danish's expertise in business and tech-related subjects is evident in his comprehensive and intuitive guides. He excels at presenting innovative ideas and futuristic trends with a grounded understanding of contemporary business needs, making his books a staple in the libraries of ambitious entrepreneurs and tech enthusiasts.

Together, Danish and Usama have cultivated a unique and diverse writing style that captivates their readers, keeping them engrossed from the first page to the last. Their books often reflect the symbiosis of their different interests and expertise, and the powerful balance between emotion and logic. Despite their varied interests, they share a commitment to creating high-quality literature that is both engaging and enlightening. The Bajwa Brothers continue to establish their presence in the literary world, building a legacy of insightful, thought-provoking, and enchanting books that truly make a difference.

Preface

Welcome to "The Art of Successful Business Software Implementation and Management." This book serves as a comprehensive guide for businesses seeking to navigate the intricacies of software implementation and management in today's dynamic and rapidly evolving digital landscape. In an era where technology plays a pivotal role in driving business success, understanding the art behind effective software initiatives is essential.

The purpose of this book is to provide readers with a holistic and practical approach to business software implementation and management. Whether you are a business owner, executive, project manager, or IT professional, the insights and strategies presented here will equip you with the necessary knowledge to embark on successful software journeys.

Software implementation and management are complex endeavors that require careful planning, strategic decision-making, and the ability to adapt to changing circumstances. This book recognizes the challenges businesses face when selecting, deploying, and managing software solutions. It aims to demystify the process and provide actionable guidance to ensure smooth and efficient software initiatives.

In the chapters ahead, we will explore various aspects of business software implementation and management, diving into topics such as planning and selecting software, user adoption, customization and optimization, security and data protection, ongoing maintenance and upgrades, project management, and emerging trends in the industry. Each chapter delves into key principles, strategies, and best practices that will empower you to navigate the software landscape with confidence and achieve success.

The chapters are organized in a logical sequence, taking you through the entire lifecycle of software implementation and management. We start by emphasizing the importance of aligning software initiatives with business goals and understanding the specific needs of your organization. Through a comprehensive assessment process, you will gain insights into the current state of your business and identify the software solutions that best fit your requirements.

Next, we delve into the critical aspect of user adoption. Implementing software is not solely about deploying a new system; it is about fostering a culture of change, engaging stakeholders, and ensuring that users embrace and utilize the software to its fullest potential. We explore strategies for effective communication, training, and change management to facilitate a smooth transition and maximize user adoption.

Customization and optimization play a pivotal role in realizing the full potential of business software. We delve into the importance of tailoring software solutions to meet specific business needs and workflows. By optimizing processes, automating repetitive tasks, and integrating software with existing systems, you can streamline operations, enhance efficiency, and achieve tangible results.

Security and data protection are paramount in today's digital landscape. As businesses increasingly rely on software solutions to store and process sensitive information, robust security measures are crucial. We discuss the implementation of security protocols, data encryption, and compliance with privacy regulations to safeguard valuable data and protect against cyber threats.

Furthermore, we explore the significance of ongoing software maintenance and upgrades. Software must evolve alongside business needs and technological advancements. We provide insights into establishing maintenance plans, performing regular updates and patches, evaluating the need for upgrades, and effectively managing software licenses and support contracts. These practices ensure the longevity, stability, and relevance of your software solutions.

Effective project management is another critical aspect of successful software initiatives. We delve into project planning, defining milestones, tracking progress, managing risks, and fostering collaboration among stakeholders. By applying project management principles, you can navigate complex software projects, stay on track, and ensure successful outcomes.

Lastly, we explore emerging trends in the industry and their potential impact on business software. Technologies such as artificial intelligence, cloud computing, Internet of Things (IoT), and blockchain are shaping the future of software solutions. We provide insights into these trends, allowing you to stay informed and prepare for the opportunities and challenges that lie ahead.

This book is not a definitive answer to every software-related challenge you may encounter. Instead, it aims to provide you with a solid foundation of knowledge and equip you with the tools and strategies necessary to embark on successful software initiatives. Each chapter presents real-world examples, case studies, and expert advice to illustrate key concepts and guide you through the process.

I encourage you to approach this book as a roadmap, adapting the principles and strategies to your unique business context. By embracing the art of successful business software implementation and management, you can unlock the potential of technology, drive innovation, and position your business for sustained growth and success in today's digital era.

Thank you for joining me on this journey. Let's begin unraveling the art behind successful business software implementation and management.

Table Of Contents

Introduction 1

Chapter 1 Understanding Business Software 5

Chapter 2 Planning and Selecting Business Software 15

Chapter 3 Implementing Business Software 28

Chapter 4 Maximizing Business Software Efficiency 44

Chapter 5 Security and Data Protection 59

Chapter 6 Maintaining and Upgrading Business Software 75

Chapter 7 Managing Business Software Projects 90

Chapter 8 Future Trends in Business Software 106

Conclusion: 126

Introduction

In today's rapidly evolving digital landscape, business software has become an indispensable tool for organizations of all sizes and industries. From streamlining operations and enhancing productivity to driving innovation and delivering exceptional customer experiences, the right software can be a game-changer. However, successfully implementing and managing business software is not just about purchasing and deploying the latest technology; it requires a strategic approach, careful planning, and a deep understanding of the art behind software initiatives.

"The Art of Business Software: A Comprehensive Guide for Success" is your essential companion on the journey to mastering the art of business software implementation and management. Whether you are a business owner, executive, project manager, or IT professional, this comprehensive guide provides you with the knowledge, insights, and strategies to navigate the complex landscape of business software effectively.

The digital transformation sweeping across industries demands a fresh perspective on software implementation. Gone are the days when software was merely a tool for automation; it has become the foundation for competitive advantage and organizational growth. As businesses strive to adapt and thrive in this digital era, understanding the importance of business software in the modern landscape is crucial.

In the opening chapters of this book, we explore the significance of business software in the modern digital landscape. We delve into the transformative impact it can have on organizations, enabling streamlined operations, data-driven decision-making, and improved customer experiences. From cloud-based solutions to mobile applications, we uncover the evolving trends shaping the future of business software, ensuring that you are prepared to leverage emerging technologies and stay ahead of the curve.

Moving forward, we delve into the crucial steps of planning and selecting business software. Implementing the right software solutions requires a deep understanding of your organization's unique needs and requirements. Through comprehensive assessments and feasibility studies, you will gain insights into the current state of your business and identify software options that align with your goals and objectives.

Effective software adoption is another vital aspect covered in this guide. Implementing software is not solely about deploying a new system; it involves a cultural shift and the art of change management. We explore strategies for effective communication, user training, and stakeholder engagement to foster a smooth transition and ensure the successful adoption of software across your organization.

Customization and optimization are key to maximizing the efficiency and impact of business software. One size does not fit all, and tailoring software solutions to meet specific business needs and workflows is critical. We delve into techniques for customizing and configuring software, empowering you to optimize processes, automate tasks, and enhance productivity. Integration with existing systems is also crucial, and we provide insights into the seamless integration of software solutions to create a unified ecosystem.

Ensuring data security and protection is paramount in today's digital landscape. With cybersecurity threats on the rise, businesses must implement robust security measures to safeguard sensitive information. We discuss best practices for data protection, encryption, access controls, and compliance with privacy regulations. By prioritizing data security, you can protect your organization's assets and maintain the trust of your customers.

Once the software is implemented, ongoing maintenance, upgrades, and performance monitoring are vital for sustained success. We explore strategies for maintaining software functionality, performing regular updates, evaluating the need for upgrades, and managing software licenses and support contracts. By adopting a proactive approach to software management, you can ensure the longevity, stability, and relevance of your software solutions.

Effective project management practices are essential for successful software initiatives. We delve into the principles of project planning, defining milestones, tracking progress, managing risks, and fostering effective communication with stakeholders. By applying these project management principles, you can effectively navigate complex software projects, meet deadlines, and achieve the desired outcomes.

Finally, we explore emerging trends in the industry and their potential impact on business software. From artificial intelligence and predictive analytics to cloud-based solutions and mobile applications, the future of software is continuously evolving. We provide insights into these trends, allowing you to stay informed and adapt your software strategies to embrace the opportunities and challenges that lie ahead.

"The Art of Business Software: A Comprehensive Guide for Success" is not just a book; it is a roadmap to navigate the intricate world of business software implementation and management.

Packed with real-world examples, case studies, and expert advice, this guide empowers you to unlock the true potential of software for your organization. By leveraging the art behind software initiatives, you can drive innovation, streamline operations, and position your business for sustained growth and success in the digital age.

Get ready to embark on a transformative journey of mastering the art of business software implementation and management. Let us delve into the intricacies of this exciting landscape together and equip ourselves with the tools and knowledge to achieve success.

Chapter 1
Understanding Business Software

In the first chapter of "The Art of Business Software: A Comprehensive Guide for Success," we embark on a journey to deepen our understanding of business software and its significance in the modern digital landscape. We begin by providing a clear definition and scope of business software, distinguishing it from consumer-oriented software applications. By doing so, readers will gain a solid foundation and a comprehensive view of the subject matter.

Next, we delve into the various types of business software and their specific applications. We explore the rich landscape of software solutions that cater to different business needs, such as Enterprise Resource Planning (ERP) systems, Customer Relationship Management (CRM) software, project management tools, accounting and financial software, supply chain management systems, Human Resources Information Systems (HRIS), and business intelligence and analytics platforms. By understanding these different types of software and their respective functions, readers will gain insights into the breadth and diversity of options available to address specific organizational requirements.

Having established the landscape of business software, we then examine the benefits and challenges associated with its utilization. We delve into the advantages that business software brings to organizations, including increased operational efficiency and productivity, improved accuracy and reduced errors, enhanced data management and reporting capabilities, streamlined communication and collaboration, and facilitated decision-making based on real-time insights. At the same time, we acknowledge the challenges organizations may encounter during the adoption and implementation of business software, such as initial implementation costs, integration with existing systems, data security and privacy concerns, and potential resistance from users. By understanding these benefits and challenges, readers can navigate the landscape of business software more effectively and make informed decisions.

Lastly, we turn our attention to the evolving nature of business software. We explore the latest trends and developments that shape the software industry, such as cloud-based solutions and the rise of Software-as-a-Service (SaaS) models, the impact of mobile applications on business software, the integration of artificial intelligence and machine learning into software automation and decision-making processes, the role of blockchain technology in enhancing security and transparency, and emerging software categories and innovations. By discussing these trends, readers gain insights into the evolving nature of business software and the potential opportunities and challenges that lie ahead.

In conclusion, Chapter 1 serves as a comprehensive introduction to the world of business software. It provides readers with a solid understanding of the definition, types, benefits, and challenges associated with business software. By establishing this understanding, readers are well-prepared to dive deeper into subsequent chapters, which will explore topics such as planning and selecting business software, implementing and maximizing software efficiency, ensuring security and data protection, managing software projects, and embracing future trends. Armed with this knowledge, readers will be equipped to navigate the complex landscape of business software and harness its full potential for organizational success.

Business software refers to a broad category of computer programs and applications specifically designed to facilitate and enhance various aspects of business operations. It encompasses a wide range of software solutions that cater to the diverse needs of organizations, regardless of their size or industry. Unlike consumer-oriented software, business software is developed with the primary goal of improving efficiency, productivity, and overall performance within the context of a business environment.

The scope of business software is expansive, covering a multitude of functions and processes across different departments and disciplines within an organization. It encompasses software applications that address areas such as:

Enterprise Resource Planning (ERP)

ERP software integrates and manages core business processes such as accounting, human resources, inventory management, supply chain management, and customer relationship management. It provides a centralized system for data and workflow management, enabling organizations to streamline their operations, enhance collaboration, and improve decision-making.

Customer Relationship Management (CRM)

CRM software is designed to help organizations effectively manage interactions and relationships with customers. It provides tools for tracking customer interactions, managing sales pipelines, automating marketing campaigns, and generating analytics to optimize customer engagement and retention.

Project Management

Project management software facilitates the planning, coordination, and execution of projects within an organization. It helps teams collaborate, assign tasks, track progress, manage resources, and monitor timelines, ensuring projects are completed efficiently and within budget.

Accounting and Financial Software

Accounting software simplifies financial management tasks such as bookkeeping, invoicing, payroll processing, and financial reporting. It automates calculations, tracks expenses, generates financial statements, and ensures compliance with tax regulations.

Human Resources Information Systems (HRIS)

HRIS software streamlines human resources processes, including employee onboarding, attendance tracking, benefits administration, performance management, and employee data management. It enables organizations to centralize HR functions, enhance employee engagement, and support strategic workforce planning.

Business Intelligence and Analytics

Business intelligence software gathers, analyzes, and visualizes data to provide meaningful insights into business performance. It enables organizations to make data-driven decisions, identify trends, forecast outcomes, and optimize operations based on actionable information.

Supply Chain Management (SCM)

SCM software optimizes the flow of goods and services throughout the supply chain, from procurement to production and distribution. It helps organizations manage inventory levels, track shipments, improve logistics, and enhance collaboration with suppliers and partners.

The scope of business software extends beyond these examples, as there are specialized software solutions tailored to specific industries and functions. It continues to evolve as new technologies emerge, enabling organizations to leverage advanced capabilities such as artificial intelligence, machine learning, cloud computing, and mobile applications to further enhance their operations.

In summary, the definition and scope of business software encompass a wide array of specialized applications designed to support and streamline various aspects of business operations. From ERP and CRM systems to project management and business intelligence tools, business software plays a vital role in enhancing efficiency, productivity, and overall success in today's competitive business landscape.

There are various types of business software available, each designed to address specific needs and functions within an organization. Here, we explore some of the most common types of business software and their applications:

Enterprise Resource Planning (ERP) Software

ERP software integrates core business processes, including finance, human resources, inventory management, supply chain management, and customer relationship management. It provides a centralized system for data management, streamlines operations, enhances collaboration, and facilitates efficient resource utilization.

Customer Relationship Management (CRM) Software

CRM software helps businesses manage customer interactions, sales processes, and marketing campaigns. It enables organizations to track customer data, improve customer service, automate sales pipelines, analyze customer behavior, and build long-lasting customer relationships.

Project Management Software

Project management software assists in planning, organizing, and executing projects within an organization. It provides tools for task management, collaboration, resource allocation, scheduling, and progress tracking. It helps teams stay organized, meet deadlines, and ensure successful project completion.

Accounting Software

Accounting software simplifies financial management tasks such as bookkeeping, invoicing, payroll processing, and financial reporting. It automates financial calculations, tracks expenses, generates financial statements, and ensures compliance with accounting standards and tax regulations.

Human Resources Management Systems (HRMS)

HRMS software supports various HR functions, including employee data management, payroll processing, benefits administration, performance management, time and attendance tracking, and recruitment. It helps streamline HR processes, improve employee engagement, and ensure compliance with employment regulations.

Business Intelligence (BI) and Analytics Software

BI and analytics software enable organizations to collect, analyze, and visualize data to gain insights into business performance. It helps in data-driven decision-making, identifies trends and patterns, provides dashboards and reports, and facilitates strategic planning and forecasting.

Supply Chain Management (SCM) Software

SCM software optimizes the flow of goods and services across the supply chain. It includes modules for procurement, inventory management, demand forecasting, order fulfillment, and logistics. SCM software helps organizations improve efficiency, reduce costs, and enhance collaboration with suppliers and partners.

Communication and Collaboration Software

Communication and collaboration software includes tools for email, instant messaging, video conferencing, document sharing, and project collaboration. It helps teams communicate effectively, collaborate in real-time, and share information seamlessly.

E-commerce Platforms

E-commerce platforms enable businesses to establish and manage online stores, process online transactions, and manage inventory and customer orders. They provide features for product catalog management, shopping cart functionality, secure payment processing, and order fulfillment.

Business Process Management (BPM) Software

BPM software helps organizations model, automate, and optimize their business processes. It allows businesses to document workflows, automate routine tasks, track progress, and analyze process efficiency to drive operational improvements.

These are just a few examples of the many types of business software available. As technology continues to advance, new software categories and specialized solutions emerge to address specific industry needs and challenges. Choosing the right software solutions and effectively integrating them into business processes can greatly enhance efficiency, productivity, and competitiveness in today's dynamic business landscape.

Business software offers several benefits that contribute to increased efficiency, productivity, and competitiveness. However, it also presents certain challenges that organizations need to address for successful implementation and utilization. Let's explore the benefits and challenges of using business software:

Benefits of Using Business Software

Increased Operational Efficiency

Business software automates manual tasks, streamlines processes, and reduces human error, leading to improved efficiency and productivity. It eliminates repetitive and time-consuming activities, allowing employees to focus on more value-added tasks.

Improved Decision-Making

Business software provides access to real-time data and analytics, enabling informed decision-making. It generates reports, visualizations, and insights that assist in evaluating performance, identifying trends, and forecasting outcomes. Data-driven decision-making leads to better strategic choices.

Enhanced Collaboration and Communication

Business software often includes collaboration tools and centralized platforms for communication. It facilitates effective team collaboration, knowledge sharing, and seamless communication across departments and geographies. This fosters collaboration, improves teamwork, and accelerates project completion.

Better Customer Relationship Management

Customer relationship management software helps businesses understand customer needs, track interactions, and provide personalized experiences. It enables organizations to manage customer data, automate sales processes, and deliver exceptional customer service, resulting in increased customer satisfaction and loyalty.

Streamlined Business Processes

Business software standardizes and automates workflows, ensuring consistent and efficient processes. It reduces manual errors, eliminates redundant steps, and enables the optimization of business processes, leading to increased productivity and cost savings.

Challenges of Using Business Software

Implementation Costs and Complexity

Implementing business software often requires significant upfront investment in licenses, hardware, and infrastructure. It may also involve training employees and adapting existing processes, which can be complex and time-consuming.

Integration with Existing Systems

Integrating new software with existing systems can be challenging, especially when dealing with legacy or customized systems. Ensuring smooth data flow and compatibility between different software applications may require careful planning and technical expertise.

Data Security and Privacy Concerns

Business software involves the storage and processing of sensitive business and customer data. Ensuring data security and privacy protection is crucial to prevent breaches, unauthorized access, and data loss. Organizations must implement robust security measures and adhere to data protection regulations.

User Resistance and Change Management

Introducing new software can face resistance from employees who may be accustomed to existing processes. Change management efforts, including training, communication, and addressing user concerns, are essential to facilitate a smooth transition and gain user acceptance.

System Downtime and Technical Issues

Business software, like any technology, may experience downtime, software bugs, or technical glitches. Organizations need to have contingency plans, technical support, and maintenance processes in place to minimize disruptions and resolve issues promptly.

By recognizing and addressing these challenges, organizations can harness the full benefits of business software while mitigating potential risks. Thorough planning, effective change management, ongoing training, and robust technical support contribute to successful implementation and utilization of business software solutions.

Chapter 2
Planning and Selecting Business Software

In Chapter 2 of "The Art of Business Software: A Comprehensive Guide for Success," we delve into the crucial process of planning and selecting the right software for your organization. This chapter equips readers with the knowledge and strategies needed to navigate the complexities of choosing the most suitable business software solutions.

We begin by emphasizing the importance of thoroughly understanding and defining your business needs and requirements. By conducting a comprehensive assessment of your organization's processes, pain points, and goals, you can identify the specific areas where software can provide the most value. This analysis sets the foundation for selecting software that aligns with your unique business objectives.

Next, we guide readers through the process of conducting a feasibility study. This involves evaluating the technical, operational, financial, and strategic aspects of implementing new software solutions. By thoroughly assessing factors such as budget, resource availability, technical capabilities, and potential return on investment, organizations can make informed decisions about software implementation.

The chapter then delves into the evaluation and selection process. We provide readers with key considerations and best practices for assessing software options. This includes identifying critical features and functionalities, examining scalability and flexibility, evaluating vendor reputation and support, and considering factors such as integration capabilities and future upgrade paths.

To facilitate the selection process, we explore the significance of creating a software selection team comprising stakeholders from various departments within the organization. Involving individuals with diverse perspectives and expertise ensures a comprehensive evaluation of software options and improves the likelihood of selecting a solution that meets the needs of all stakeholders.

Additionally, we discuss the importance of conducting software demonstrations and trials to assess the usability, user experience, and compatibility with existing systems. This hands-on approach allows organizations to gain firsthand experience and evaluate how the software will fit within their specific environment.

Furthermore, we emphasize the value of seeking references and conducting due diligence on software vendors. By gathering feedback from current users, checking vendor credentials, and examining testimonials or case studies, organizations can gain insights into the reliability, customer support, and overall reputation of potential software providers.

Finally, we provide guidance on making the final decision and negotiating contracts with selected vendors. This includes considerations such as pricing models, licensing agreements, support and maintenance terms, implementation timelines, and service-level agreements. By carefully reviewing and negotiating these aspects, organizations can ensure a successful and mutually beneficial partnership with the chosen software vendor.

In conclusion, Chapter 2 serves as a comprehensive guide for planning and selecting business software. By understanding the importance of assessing business needs, conducting feasibility studies, evaluating software options, and involving key stakeholders, organizations can make informed decisions that align software solutions with their strategic objectives. The chapter equips readers with practical advice and best practices for navigating the software selection process, ensuring the successful adoption of software solutions that drive organizational success.

Assessing Business Needs and Requirements

One of the fundamental steps in planning and selecting business software is assessing your organization's needs and requirements. This process involves gaining a comprehensive understanding of your current operations, pain points, and goals to identify the specific areas where software can provide the most value. Here, we explore the importance of assessing business needs and offer guidance on conducting an effective assessment.

First and foremost, it is crucial to involve key stakeholders from different departments and levels within your organization. This ensures that a wide range of perspectives and insights are considered during the assessment process. By involving individuals who are directly impacted by the software or have a deep understanding of the organization's workflows, you can capture diverse requirements and foster greater buy-in throughout the implementation.

Start by mapping out your existing business processes. Document the steps involved in key workflows, identify pain points, and pinpoint areas that require improvement. This process provides a clear picture of how your organization currently operates and serves as a foundation for identifying software functionalities that can streamline and enhance these processes.

Next, define your specific goals and objectives for implementing new software. What are the desired outcomes? Are you aiming to improve operational efficiency, enhance customer service, increase sales, or streamline financial processes? By clearly defining your goals, you can focus on selecting software solutions that align with these objectives and provide the necessary features and capabilities to achieve them.

Consider the scalability and flexibility of your organization. Assess whether the software should support growth and expansion, accommodate increasing data volumes, or handle evolving business requirements. Anticipating future needs will help you select software that can adapt and scale as your organization evolves, avoiding the need for frequent software replacements.

Another critical aspect is to consider the integration requirements with your existing systems and infrastructure. Evaluate how the new software will interact with your current technology stack, databases, and tools. Determine if the software can seamlessly integrate with your systems to ensure smooth data flow and minimize disruptions.

During the assessment, it is essential to involve end-users who will be utilizing the software on a daily basis. Solicit their input to understand their pain points, challenges, and requirements. This not only ensures that their needs are considered but also helps in fostering user adoption and addressing potential resistance during the implementation process.

Consider any industry-specific compliance requirements or regulations that your organization needs to adhere to. Certain industries, such as healthcare or finance, have specific data security and privacy regulations. Ensure that the software aligns with these requirements and has the necessary safeguards in place to protect sensitive information.

Lastly, assess the budget and resources available for software implementation. Determine the financial investment required, including licensing costs, implementation fees, and ongoing maintenance expenses. Consider the availability of internal resources such as IT staff or consultants who can assist with the implementation and ongoing support.

By thoroughly assessing your organization's needs and requirements, involving key stakeholders, mapping out processes, defining goals, considering scalability, integration, user perspectives, industry compliance, and budget, you can establish a solid foundation for selecting business software that will effectively address your organization's unique needs and contribute to its overall success.

Conducting a Feasibility Study

Once you have assessed your organization's needs and identified potential software solutions, the next crucial step is conducting a feasibility study. This study evaluates the technical, operational, financial, and strategic aspects of implementing the selected software. By conducting a comprehensive feasibility study, you can make informed decisions about software implementation and ensure its success. Here, we explore the key components of a feasibility study and offer guidance on conducting it effectively.

Technical Feasibility

Assess the technical feasibility of implementing the software by evaluating factors such as compatibility with existing systems, hardware and infrastructure requirements, and technical expertise within your organization. Determine if the software can be integrated smoothly with your current technology stack and if your IT team has the necessary skills to support the implementation.

Operational Feasibility

Evaluate the operational feasibility of the software by examining how it aligns with your organization's workflows and processes. Consider whether the software can effectively streamline operations, enhance productivity, and deliver the desired outcomes. Identify any potential disruptions or challenges that may arise during the implementation process and determine how they can be mitigated.

Financial Feasibility

Assess the financial feasibility by analyzing the costs associated with implementing and maintaining the software. Consider the licensing fees, implementation expenses, hardware upgrades, training costs, and ongoing support and maintenance fees. Evaluate the potential return on investment (ROI) and determine if the financial benefits outweigh the costs over the long term.

Strategic Feasibility

Analyze the strategic feasibility by aligning the software implementation with your organization's overall goals and strategies. Determine if the software supports your strategic objectives, enhances competitiveness, and helps achieve a sustainable competitive advantage. Evaluate how the software fits within your long-term plans and if it aligns with the evolving needs of your organization.

Risk Assessment

Identify potential risks and challenges that may arise during the implementation process. Consider factors such as data security risks, system downtime, user resistance, and vendor reliability. Assess the severity and impact of these risks and develop mitigation strategies to minimize their effects on the implementation.

Stakeholder Analysis

Consider the perspectives and interests of key stakeholders who will be impacted by the software implementation. Identify their needs, concerns, and expectations. Engage with stakeholders through surveys, interviews, and workshops to ensure their input is considered in the decision-making process. Addressing stakeholder concerns early on can enhance buy-in and facilitate a smoother implementation.

Documentation and Reporting

Document all findings, analysis, and conclusions from the feasibility study in a comprehensive report. This report will serve as a reference for decision-making, as well as provide transparency and documentation throughout the implementation process. Clearly communicate the feasibility study results to key stakeholders, ensuring that they understand the implications and benefits of implementing the software.

By conducting a thorough feasibility study, you can assess the technical, operational, financial, and strategic viability of implementing the selected software. This study provides valuable insights that inform decision-making and allows organizations to anticipate and address potential challenges, thereby increasing the chances of a successful software implementation that aligns with the organization's goals and contributes to its overall success.

Evaluating Different Software Options

Once you have conducted a feasibility study and defined your organization's needs, the next step in the software selection process is evaluating different software options. This evaluation phase is critical as it enables you to compare and assess various solutions to determine the best fit for your organization. Here, we explore key considerations and best practices for effectively evaluating different software options.

Identify Key Features and Functionalities

Start by identifying the key features and functionalities that are essential for addressing your organization's needs. Create a list of specific requirements and prioritize them based on their importance. This ensures that you focus on solutions that offer the necessary capabilities to support your operations and achieve your goals.

Scalability and Flexibility

Consider the scalability and flexibility of the software options. Assess whether they can accommodate your organization's growth and changing needs. Determine if the software can scale with your business, handle increasing data volumes, and adapt to evolving requirements. This ensures that the software can support your organization's long-term goals and future expansion.

Integration Capabilities

Evaluate the integration capabilities of each software option. Consider how well the software can integrate with your existing systems, databases, and tools. Assess whether it can seamlessly exchange data and information with other applications, ensuring smooth interoperability. Robust integration capabilities prevent data silos and enable efficient data flow across your organization.

User Experience and Usability

Assess the user experience and usability of each software option. Consider how intuitive and user-friendly the interface is. Look for software that minimizes the learning curve and offers a pleasant user experience. Conduct software demonstrations or request trials to gain firsthand experience and evaluate how easily your team can adapt to and utilize the software.

Vendor Reputation and Support

Research and evaluate the reputation and credibility of software vendors. Consider factors such as the vendor's experience, industry presence, and customer reviews. Look for vendors who have a track record of providing reliable and high-quality software solutions. Additionally, assess the level of support and customer service offered by the vendor to ensure that you receive timely assistance when needed.

Total Cost of Ownership

Consider the total cost of ownership (TCO) of each software option. Evaluate not only the upfront costs but also ongoing expenses, such as licensing fees, maintenance and support fees, and any additional costs for customization or integration. Compare the TCO of different options to ensure that they align with your budget and provide a satisfactory ROI.

Future Upgrade Paths and Roadmap

Assess the future upgrade paths and roadmap of the software options. Consider how frequently the vendor releases updates and new features. Evaluate their commitment to staying current with industry trends and evolving technologies. Look for software that offers a clear product roadmap, indicating ongoing development and enhancements to meet your organization's evolving needs.

References and Case Studies

Request references from the software vendors and speak to their existing customers. This allows you to gather feedback on the software's performance, reliability, and vendor support. Additionally, review case studies or success stories to understand how other organizations have benefited from implementing the software. Insights from references and case studies provide valuable real-world experiences to inform your decision-making process.

By thoroughly evaluating different software options based on key features, scalability, integration capabilities, user experience, vendor reputation, total cost of ownership, future upgrade paths, and references, you can make an informed decision. It is important to involve key stakeholders in the evaluation process and consider their perspectives and requirements. Remember that selecting the right software solution requires careful consideration and analysis to ensure a successful implementation that meets your organization's needs and drives its overall success.

Making Informed Decisions and Selecting the Right Software

Selecting the right software for your organization is a critical decision that can have a profound impact on your operations and overall success. By following a systematic approach and considering key factors, you can make informed decisions and choose the software that best aligns with your organization's needs. Here, we explore best practices for selecting the right software and ensuring a successful implementation.

Evaluate Alignment with Business Needs

Review your organization's needs and requirements in detail, considering the findings from your assessment and feasibility study. Ensure that the software solution aligns closely with your specific business needs and addresses the pain points you identified. Prioritize the software options that offer the most comprehensive coverage of your requirements.

Involve Key Stakeholders

Engage key stakeholders from various departments in the decision-making process. This includes end-users, managers, IT personnel, and executive leadership. Each stakeholder group may have unique perspectives and requirements. Involving them in the evaluation and decision-making process helps foster buy-in, enhances user adoption, and ensures that the selected software meets the needs of all stakeholders.

Conduct Software Demonstrations and Trials

Request software demonstrations from the shortlisted vendors. These demonstrations provide an opportunity to evaluate the software's user interface, functionality, and ease of use. If possible, request trials or pilot programs to test the software in a real-world scenario. This hands-on experience enables you to assess how well the software aligns with your workflows and if it meets your expectations.

Consider Integration and Scalability

Assess how well the software integrates with your existing systems and databases. Determine if it offers the flexibility to scale and adapt as your organization grows and evolves. Consider the potential future integration needs and ensure that the software can seamlessly connect with other applications critical to your business processes.

Evaluate Vendor Support and Reputation

Research the reputation and reliability of the software vendors. Consider factors such as their industry experience, customer reviews, and track record of providing timely and effective support. Evaluate the vendor's commitment to ongoing support, including regular updates, bug fixes, and customer assistance. Choose a vendor known for their customer-centric approach and long-term partnership.

Review Total Cost of Ownership (TCO)

Consider the total cost of ownership (TCO) of the software, including upfront costs, ongoing licensing fees, maintenance and support fees, training expenses, and potential customization or integration costs. Compare the TCO of different options and evaluate their value proposition in relation to the benefits and ROI they offer. Ensure that the selected software fits within your budget and provides a satisfactory return on investment.

Seek References and Case Studies

Request references from the software vendors and contact their existing customers. Obtain feedback on their experience with the software, including implementation process, vendor support, and overall satisfaction. Review case studies or success stories to understand how similar organizations have benefited from using the software. Insights from references and case studies can help validate the vendor's claims and provide valuable real-world perspectives.

Make a Well-Informed Decision

Based on the evaluation, stakeholder input, vendor reputation, TCO analysis, and references, make a well-informed decision. Select the software that best aligns with your organization's needs, demonstrates reliability and scalability, offers robust support, and provides a strong fit with your long-term goals and strategic vision. Document the decision-making process, including the rationale behind the selection, to ensure transparency and maintain a record of the decision for future reference.

By following these best practices and conducting a thorough evaluation, you can select the right software that meets your organization's needs and sets the stage for a successful implementation. Remember that software selection is an iterative process that requires collaboration, research, and careful consideration. With a well-informed decision, you can leverage the chosen software

Chapter 3
Implementing Business Software

In Chapter 3 of "The Art of Business Software: A Comprehensive Guide for Success," we delve into the critical phase of implementing business software. This chapter focuses on the practical aspects of successfully introducing and integrating the chosen software solution into your organization's operations. By following best practices and effective strategies, you can maximize the benefits of the software and ensure a smooth implementation process.

We begin by emphasizing the importance of proper preparation before initiating the implementation. This involves establishing a clear implementation plan with defined objectives, timelines, and key milestones. It is essential to engage stakeholders and communicate the implementation plan across the organization, ensuring everyone understands their roles and responsibilities throughout the process.

Next, we discuss the significance of data migration and preparation. Smooth and accurate data transfer is crucial for a successful implementation. We guide readers on evaluating their existing data, cleansing and organizing it, and determining the most effective migration strategy. By ensuring the quality and integrity of the data, organizations can avoid potential issues and maximize the software's effectiveness.

The chapter then delves into the importance of change management during the implementation process. Introducing new software often brings changes to established workflows, processes, and routines. We provide strategies for managing change, including effective communication, engaging end-users in the process, providing training and support, and addressing resistance. By focusing on change management, organizations can foster user adoption and minimize disruptions during the transition.

Furthermore, we explore the significance of customization and configuration to align the software with the organization's specific requirements. We discuss the available customization options, best practices for tailoring the software to fit organizational needs, and considerations for striking the right balance between customization and maintaining the integrity of the software.

Effective training is another crucial aspect of implementing business software. We emphasize the need for comprehensive and ongoing training programs to ensure users have the necessary skills and knowledge to utilize the software effectively. We discuss different training approaches, such as on-site training, online tutorials, documentation, and knowledge-sharing sessions. By investing in training, organizations can empower their employees and maximize the software's potential.

The chapter also addresses the significance of monitoring and evaluating the implementation process. Regularly assessing the progress, identifying challenges, and measuring the software's impact are critical for making necessary adjustments and ensuring a successful implementation. We discuss key performance indicators (KPIs) and metrics that can be used to track the software's effectiveness and measure its impact on key business outcomes.

Lastly, we highlight the importance of ongoing support and maintenance after the initial implementation. Software requires regular updates, bug fixes, and technical support to ensure its optimal performance. We discuss the significance of maintaining a strong relationship with the software vendor, exploring available support channels, and establishing procedures for handling software issues and updates.

In conclusion, Chapter 3 provides readers with practical guidance for successfully implementing business software. By emphasizing the importance of preparation, data migration, change management, customization, training, monitoring, and ongoing support, organizations can navigate the implementation process effectively. Implementing business software requires a holistic approach that encompasses not only the technical aspects but also the people, processes, and organizational change. With the right strategies and a well-executed implementation plan, organizations can leverage the full potential of the software and drive positive outcomes.

Preparing for Software Implementation

Before embarking on the implementation of business software, it is essential to undertake thorough preparation to set the stage for a successful implementation process. Chapter 3 of "The Art of Business Software: A Comprehensive Guide for Success" emphasizes the significance of proper preparation and provides valuable insights on the essential steps involved. Here, we explore the key aspects of preparing for software implementation.

Establish Clear Objectives and Goals

Clearly define the objectives and goals of the software implementation. What specific outcomes are you aiming to achieve? Are you seeking to improve operational efficiency, enhance customer service, or streamline financial processes? By establishing clear objectives, you can align the implementation process with your organization's strategic priorities and ensure that the software serves its intended purpose.

Develop an Implementation Plan

Create a comprehensive implementation plan that outlines the steps, timelines, and key milestones of the implementation process. Identify the resources and personnel required for each stage and allocate responsibilities accordingly. This plan acts as a roadmap, guiding the implementation team and stakeholders through the process and ensuring a structured and organized approach to implementation.

Engage Stakeholders

Involve key stakeholders throughout the implementation process. This includes end-users, managers, IT personnel, and executive leadership. Ensure that all stakeholders have a voice and their perspectives are considered. Engaging stakeholders early on fosters buy-in, creates a sense of ownership, and increases the chances of successful user adoption.

Establish Communication Channels

Establish effective communication channels to keep stakeholders informed and engaged throughout the implementation process. Regularly communicate the progress, milestones achieved, and any changes or updates related to the implementation. Transparent and timely communication fosters trust, manages expectations, and mitigates resistance or misunderstandings.

Prepare Data Migration and Clean-up

Evaluate your existing data and determine the data migration strategy. Identify the necessary data to be migrated, ensuring its accuracy, completeness, and consistency. Cleanse and organize the data to avoid transferring any redundant or erroneous information. This step ensures a smooth transition and allows for the effective utilization of the software's features and functionalities.

Consider Infrastructure and Hardware Requirements

Assess your organization's infrastructure and hardware requirements for the software implementation. Ensure that your existing systems can support the software and meet its technical specifications. If necessary, upgrade your hardware or make infrastructure adjustments to optimize performance and compatibility.

Allocate Resources

Allocate the necessary resources, including personnel, budget, and time, for the implementation process. Ensure that the implementation team has the required skills and expertise to effectively carry out their roles. Adequate resource allocation and planning minimize disruptions and enable a more efficient implementation.

Develop a Training Program

Implement a comprehensive training program to equip end-users with the knowledge and skills to utilize the software effectively. Tailor the training program to address the specific needs of different user groups. Consider a combination of training methods, such as workshops, online tutorials, documentation, and hands-on practice.

Training ensures a smoother transition, boosts user confidence, and maximizes the benefits of the software.

Test and Validate

Conduct thorough testing of the software before the full implementation to identify and resolve any issues or bugs. Validate the software's performance, functionality, and compatibility within your organization's environment. User acceptance testing (UAT) involving representative end-users can help ensure that the software meets their specific needs and requirements.

Establish Post-Implementation Support

Develop a plan for post-implementation support and maintenance. Determine how software issues, questions, and updates will be addressed. Establish support channels, such as a help desk or dedicated support team, to provide timely assistance to end-users. Ongoing support and maintenance ensure the longevity and optimal performance of the software.

By following these key steps in preparing for software implementation, organizations can lay a solid foundation for a successful implementation process. Proper preparation enhances the effectiveness of the software, minimizes risks, and increases user acceptance. A well-prepared implementation process sets the stage for leveraging the full potential of the software to achieve organizational goals and drive success.

Developing an Implementation Strategy and Timeline

When preparing for software implementation, developing a clear and well-defined implementation strategy and timeline is crucial. A comprehensive strategy outlines the necessary steps, assigns responsibilities, and establishes a timeline for the successful deployment of the software. In this section, we explore the key considerations and best practices for developing an effective implementation strategy and timeline.

Define Implementation Goals

Begin by clearly defining the goals and objectives of the implementation. What specific outcomes do you want to achieve? Determine the key performance indicators (KPIs) that will measure the success of the implementation. These goals will guide the development of your implementation strategy.

Identify Critical Tasks and Milestones

Identify the critical tasks required to complete the implementation successfully. Break down the implementation process into manageable phases or stages. Each phase should have specific milestones that mark the completion of key deliverables or achievements. This allows for better monitoring of progress and ensures a structured approach to the implementation.

Assign Responsibilities

Assign clear responsibilities to individuals or teams involved in the implementation process. Identify key stakeholders, including project managers, IT personnel, end-users, and trainers. Clearly define the roles and responsibilities of each stakeholder to ensure accountability and effective coordination.

Determine Resource Requirements

Evaluate the resources needed for the implementation, including personnel, budget, infrastructure, and time. Assess whether you have the necessary resources in-house or if external support is required.

Adequately allocating resources ensures that the implementation proceeds smoothly and minimizes any potential bottlenecks.

Consider Dependencies and Interactions

Identify any dependencies or interactions between tasks and stakeholders. Determine if certain tasks need to be completed before others can begin, or if specific stakeholders' input is required at different stages. Understanding these dependencies helps you sequence tasks properly and ensures efficient collaboration and communication.

Develop a Realistic Timeline

Create a realistic timeline that outlines the start and end dates for each task or phase of the implementation. Consider the complexity of the software, the availability of resources, and potential challenges or risks that may impact the timeline. It is important to set realistic expectations and allow sufficient time for testing, training, and adjustments.

Incorporate Change Management

Integrate change management strategies into the implementation strategy and timeline. Change management involves preparing stakeholders for the upcoming changes, addressing concerns, and ensuring a smooth transition. Plan for communication, training, and support activities to facilitate user acceptance and minimize resistance.

Monitor and Adjust

Regularly monitor the progress of the implementation against the established timeline. Track the completion of tasks, milestones, and KPIs. This allows you to identify any delays or deviations and take corrective actions as needed. Flexibility is key, as adjustments to the timeline may be required to address unforeseen circumstances or changes in priorities.

Communicate and Engage Stakeholders

Maintain open and transparent communication with all stakeholders throughout the implementation process. Provide regular updates on progress, milestones achieved, and any adjustments to the timeline. Engage stakeholders through workshops, meetings, and training sessions to ensure their involvement and address any concerns or feedback.

Document and Evaluate

Document the implementation strategy and timeline, capturing all important details, decisions, and adjustments made throughout the process. This serves as a reference for future implementations or for addressing any post-implementation issues. After the implementation is completed, evaluate the effectiveness of the strategy and timeline to identify lessons learned and areas for improvement.

By developing a comprehensive implementation strategy and timeline, organizations can ensure a structured and successful deployment of the software. Clear goals, assigned responsibilities, realistic timelines, and effective communication contribute to a smoother implementation process, user acceptance, and the achievement of desired outcomes.

Managing Change and Overcoming Resistance

Implementing new business software often requires managing change within an organization. Change management is crucial to ensure a smooth transition, minimize resistance, and maximize user adoption. In this section, we explore key strategies and best practices for managing change and overcoming resistance during the software implementation process.

Communicate the Vision

Clearly communicate the vision and benefits of the software implementation to all stakeholders. Articulate how the software aligns with the organization's strategic goals and how it will improve efficiency, productivity, or customer service. Create a compelling narrative that highlights the positive impact the software will have on individuals and the organization as a whole.

Engage Stakeholders

Engage stakeholders throughout the implementation process. Involve key individuals from different departments and levels within the organization. Seek their input, address their concerns, and actively involve them in decision-making and planning. This participatory approach builds a sense of ownership and fosters buy-in, making stakeholders more receptive to the changes brought about by the software.

Provide Adequate Training and Support

Invest in comprehensive training programs to ensure that end-users have the necessary skills to effectively use the software. Tailor training programs to different user groups and provide ongoing support to address any questions or issues that arise. Empowering users with the knowledge and resources they need builds confidence and minimizes resistance.

Address Concerns and Benefits

Actively listen to concerns and address them in a timely manner. Create channels for feedback and provide forums for open discussion. Communicate the benefits of the software and how it addresses specific pain points or improves processes. Highlight success stories or case studies from other organizations that have successfully implemented similar software solutions.

Identify Change Champions

Identify individuals or teams who are enthusiastic about the software implementation and can act as change champions within the organization. These champions can help drive adoption, provide peer support, and share their positive experiences with others. Recognize and reward their efforts to further motivate them and inspire others.

Customize and Adapt

Consider customization options within the software to accommodate specific user needs or existing workflows. Tailor the software to fit the unique requirements of the organization, if feasible. Adapting the software to align with familiar processes reduces resistance and makes the transition smoother for end-users.

Lead by Example

Leadership plays a crucial role in managing change. Leaders should visibly support the software implementation and actively use it themselves. Leading by example demonstrates commitment and encourages others to embrace the change. Regularly communicate the benefits and progress of the implementation, reinforcing the importance of the software to the organization's success.

Continuous Communication

Maintain continuous and transparent communication throughout the implementation process. Regularly update stakeholders on the progress, milestones achieved, and any adjustments to the timeline. Address concerns promptly and provide timely information to keep everyone informed and engaged. Foster a culture of open communication where employees feel comfortable expressing their thoughts and concerns.

Monitor and Adapt

Monitor the implementation process and be open to making necessary adjustments based on feedback and evolving needs. Continuously evaluate the effectiveness of the software and its impact on the organization. Solicit feedback from end-users and make incremental improvements to enhance usability and address any remaining resistance.

Celebrate Success

Acknowledge and celebrate milestones and achievements throughout the implementation process. Recognize individuals or teams for their contributions and successes. Celebrating success fosters a positive environment, reinforces the value of the software, and motivates others to embrace the change.

By implementing these strategies, organizations can effectively manage change and overcome resistance during the software implementation process. Engaging stakeholders, providing training and support, addressing concerns, and fostering a positive and supportive culture contribute to successful user adoption and the realization of the software's benefits.

Ensuring Successful Adoption and User Training

A critical aspect of software implementation is ensuring successful adoption and providing effective user training. To maximize the benefits of the software and facilitate a smooth transition, organizations should focus on strategies that promote user acceptance, engagement, and proficiency. In this section, we explore key practices to ensure successful adoption and effective user training during the software implementation process.

Develop a Comprehensive Training Program

Create a well-structured and comprehensive training program that caters to the needs of different user groups within the organization. Consider various learning styles and preferences by offering a mix of training methods such as instructor-led sessions, online tutorials, self-paced modules, and hands-on practice. The training program should cover both basic functionalities and advanced features, ensuring users are equipped with the necessary skills to utilize the software effectively.

Tailor Training to User Roles and Responsibilities

Customize training sessions to align with the specific roles and responsibilities of different user groups. Focus on the functionalities and workflows that are relevant to their job functions. By providing targeted training, users can understand how the software relates to their work and see its value in improving their daily tasks and processes.

Engage End-Users in the Training Process

Involve end-users in the training process from the early stages. Seek their input and insights on their training needs, challenges, and expectations. Actively engage them in discussions, demonstrations, and hands-on exercises during training sessions. Encouraging active participation creates a sense of ownership and builds confidence among users.

Provide Hands-On Practice and Real-Life Scenarios

Ensure that training includes hands-on practice with the software. Offer real-life scenarios and simulations that reflect the users' day-to-day work environment. This practical approach allows users to apply their newly acquired knowledge, gain confidence, and understand how the software supports their specific tasks and processes.

Foster a Continuous Learning Culture

Promote a culture of continuous learning beyond the initial training sessions. Provide resources such as user manuals, online help guides, and knowledge bases that users can access whenever they need assistance or to refresh their knowledge. Encourage users to share tips, tricks, and best practices with their peers, fostering a collaborative learning environment.

Offer Ongoing Support

Ensure that users have access to ongoing support channels. Establish a dedicated help desk or support team to address user questions and concerns in a timely manner. Encourage users to reach out for assistance whenever needed, and provide clear guidelines on how to access support resources. Prompt and effective support boosts user confidence and minimizes frustration.

Communicate the Benefits and Impact

Continuously communicate the benefits of the software and highlight its impact on individuals, teams, and the organization as a whole. Reinforce how the software streamlines processes, improves efficiency, and enhances outcomes. Sharing success stories and showcasing examples of how the software has solved specific challenges can motivate users and reinforce their commitment to adopting and utilizing the software effectively.

Monitor User Progress and Provide Feedback

Regularly monitor user progress and provide constructive feedback. Offer guidance on how to maximize the software's potential and optimize their workflows. Conduct periodic assessments or surveys to gauge user satisfaction, identify areas for improvement, and gather suggestions for enhancing the training program or addressing any remaining barriers to adoption.

Encourage Peer Support and Mentoring

Facilitate peer support and mentoring among users. Encourage experienced users to share their knowledge and provide guidance to others. Establish forums or discussion boards where users can ask questions, share experiences, and learn from each other. Peer support fosters a sense of community, reduces reliance on formal support channels, and encourages continuous learning.

Evaluate Training Effectiveness

Regularly evaluate the effectiveness of the training program and make necessary adjustments based on user feedback and evolving needs. Analyze metrics such as user proficiency, system usage, and user satisfaction to assess the impact of the training. Use this feedback to enhance future training initiatives and ensure continuous improvement.

By implementing these practices, organizations can promote successful adoption of the software and empower users to become proficient in its usage. Effective training programs, ongoing support, engagement, and communication of benefits contribute to user satisfaction, increased productivity, and the realization of the software's full potential within the organization.

Chapter 4
Maximizing Business Software Efficiency

In Chapter 4 of "The Art of Business Software: A Comprehensive Guide for Success," we delve into the strategies and best practices for maximizing the efficiency of business software. This chapter focuses on optimizing the usage of the software to enhance productivity, streamline processes, and drive overall organizational efficiency. By implementing the techniques discussed in this chapter, businesses can unlock the full potential of their software investments.

The chapter begins by emphasizing the importance of aligning the software with organizational goals and workflows. It highlights the need for a deep understanding of the software's capabilities and features to identify opportunities for optimization. By aligning the software with specific business objectives, organizations can leverage its functionalities to achieve greater efficiency in various areas of operation.

Next, the chapter explores the significance of customization and configuration options within the software. It provides insights into tailoring the software to align with unique business requirements and processes. By customizing the software, organizations can optimize workflows, automate repetitive tasks, and improve overall efficiency. It also offers guidance on striking the right balance between customization and maintaining the integrity of the software.

The chapter then delves into data management strategies. It highlights the importance of clean and accurate data for optimal software efficiency. It covers topics such as data governance, data cleansing, and data integration to ensure that the software operates with reliable and consistent data. Effective data management not only enhances the accuracy of reports and analytics but also enables efficient decision-making and improved overall performance.

Furthermore, the chapter explores the integration capabilities of the software. It emphasizes the benefits of integrating the software with other relevant systems and applications within the organization's technology ecosystem. Seamless integration facilitates data exchange, eliminates manual data entry, and enables real-time information sharing, leading to improved efficiency and data accuracy across different functions and departments.

The chapter also discusses the significance of process optimization and automation. It explores techniques such as workflow analysis, identifying bottlenecks, and streamlining processes through automation. By leveraging the software's automation features, organizations can eliminate manual tasks, reduce errors, and accelerate process execution, ultimately improving overall efficiency and productivity.

Moreover, the chapter highlights the value of continuous learning and staying updated with software enhancements and new features. It emphasizes the need for ongoing training and knowledge-sharing initiatives to ensure that users are proficient in utilizing the software's full potential. By promoting continuous learning, organizations can stay abreast of industry best practices and leverage the latest software functionalities to optimize efficiency.

The chapter concludes by emphasizing the importance of monitoring and evaluating the software's performance. It discusses key performance indicators (KPIs) and metrics that organizations can use to assess the efficiency and impact of the software. By regularly monitoring and evaluating performance, organizations can identify areas for improvement, make informed decisions, and further optimize their software usage.

In summary, Chapter 4 provides readers with practical strategies and best practices for maximizing the efficiency of business software. By aligning the software with organizational goals, customizing it to fit specific requirements, managing data effectively, optimizing processes, embracing automation, promoting continuous learning, and monitoring performance, organizations can unlock the full potential of their software investments and drive increased efficiency and productivity throughout the organization.

Customizing and Configuring Software to Meet Specific Business Needs:Understand Your Business Requirements

Start by gaining a deep understanding of your organization's specific business requirements. Identify the pain points, challenges, and opportunities for improvement within your workflows and processes. Engage key stakeholders to gather insights and perspectives that will inform the customization and configuration process.

Identify Customization Options

Thoroughly explore the customization options available within the software. This may include features, modules, templates, or settings that can be adjusted to align with your organization's needs.

Identify which elements of the software can be customized and determine the extent to which they can be modified.

Prioritize Customization Efforts

Prioritize customization efforts based on the significance of the requirements and their potential impact on improving efficiency and productivity. Focus on areas that offer the highest value or where customization can streamline critical processes, enhance data accuracy, or deliver a competitive advantage. This helps allocate resources effectively and ensures that customization efforts address the most crucial needs.

Engage with Software Vendor or IT Team

Collaborate with the software vendor or your internal IT team to understand the customization capabilities and seek their expertise. They can provide guidance on the feasibility of customization options, best practices, and potential implications. Work closely with them to ensure that the customization aligns with the software's capabilities and does not compromise its stability or future updates.

Test and Validate Customizations

Before deploying customized changes in a live environment, thoroughly test and validate them in a controlled setting. Conduct extensive testing to ensure that the customized elements function as intended and do not introduce unintended consequences or conflicts with other system components. Test with representative user scenarios and gather feedback to make any necessary adjustments before implementation.

Document Customization Decisions

Document all customization decisions, including the rationale, process, and specific changes made. This documentation serves as a reference for future updates, maintenance, and troubleshooting. It provides transparency and ensures that the knowledge regarding customizations is preserved within the organization.

Regularly Review and Adapt Customizations

As your organization evolves and business needs change, regularly review and adapt the customizations to ensure their continued relevance and effectiveness. Stay informed about software updates and new features released by the vendor. Evaluate if existing customizations need modification or if new customization opportunities arise to better align the software with evolving business requirements.

Strike a Balance

While customization is important, it is essential to strike a balance between tailoring the software and maintaining its core integrity. Consider the long-term implications of customization on software stability, compatibility with future upgrades, and ongoing support. Avoid excessive customization that may hinder the software's ability to evolve or create dependencies that are difficult to manage.

Promote User Adoption and Training

Ensure that end-users receive adequate training and support to effectively utilize the customized software. Offer training programs that specifically address the customized elements and highlight their benefits. Promote awareness and communicate the value of the customizations to foster user acceptance and engagement.

Evaluate the Impact

Regularly evaluate the impact of the customizations on efficiency and productivity. Use key performance indicators (KPIs) and metrics to assess how the customized software has improved workflows, reduced manual efforts, or enhanced outcomes. Analyze the data to identify any further opportunities for customization or optimization.

By following these best practices, organizations can effectively customize and configure software to meet specific business needs. Tailoring the software to align with unique requirements enhances efficiency, streamlines processes, and empowers organizations to derive maximum value from their software investments.

Optimizing Software Workflows and Processes

Optimizing software workflows and processes is a crucial step in maximizing efficiency and productivity within an organization. Chapter 4 of "The Art of Business Software: A Comprehensive Guide for Success" delves into strategies and best practices for optimizing workflows and processes to leverage the full potential of business software. In this section, we explore key approaches to optimizing software workflows and processes.

Analyze Existing Workflows

Start by analyzing your existing workflows and processes. Identify bottlenecks, inefficiencies, and areas where manual efforts can be reduced. Gain a thorough understanding of how tasks and information flow through different stages and departments. This analysis helps pinpoint areas for improvement and forms the foundation for optimizing workflows.

Identify Automation Opportunities

Identify opportunities for automation within your workflows. Look for repetitive or time-consuming tasks that can be automated through the software. Automating routine processes not only reduces manual effort but also minimizes errors and accelerates task completion. Evaluate the software's automation capabilities and explore how they can be applied to streamline workflows.

Streamline and Standardize Processes

Streamline and standardize processes to eliminate redundant steps and ensure consistency across the organization. Simplify complex workflows by removing unnecessary approvals, handovers, or paperwork. Establish clear guidelines and standard operating procedures (SOPs) to ensure that tasks are performed consistently and efficiently. The software can be configured to enforce adherence to standardized processes.

Leverage Collaboration Features

Utilize collaboration features within the software to streamline communication and collaboration among team members. Encourage real-time collaboration, file sharing, and document management through built-in collaboration tools. This reduces delays, improves decision-making, and facilitates seamless information sharing, leading to more efficient workflows.

Customize Workflows to Fit Your Organization

Customize the software's workflow capabilities to align with your organization's unique requirements. Adapt the predefined workflows to suit your specific processes or create custom workflows that reflect your organization's preferred way of working. Tailoring the software to fit your organization ensures that it supports and enhances your workflows, resulting in improved efficiency.

Implement Data Integration

Integrate data sources and systems to ensure seamless flow of information across different software applications. Identify areas where data integration can optimize workflows by reducing manual data entry or eliminating duplicate data entry. Real-time data integration ensures that information is up to date and readily available to users, enabling faster decision-making and streamlined processes.

Monitor and Measure Performance

Establish key performance indicators (KPIs) to monitor the performance of your optimized workflows. Track metrics such as cycle time, task completion rates, and resource utilization. Regularly analyze the data and identify areas for further optimization. This iterative approach allows you to continuously refine and improve your workflows to maximize efficiency.

Provide Continuous Training and Support

Ensure that users receive ongoing training and support to effectively utilize the optimized workflows. Offer training programs that familiarize users with the new processes and provide guidance on using the software to its full potential. Provide continuous support through help desks, online resources, and knowledge-sharing platforms. Regularly seek feedback from users to identify any challenges or areas for improvement.

Embrace Continuous Improvement

Adopt a mindset of continuous improvement when it comes to optimizing workflows and processes. Encourage employees to suggest ideas for process enhancements and provide a platform for sharing best practices. Regularly review and evaluate the effectiveness of the optimized workflows, identify areas for further improvement, and implement iterative changes to drive ongoing efficiency gains.

Foster a Culture of Collaboration and Innovation

Promote a culture of collaboration and innovation within your organization. Encourage cross-functional teams to work together, share ideas, and collaborate on process improvement initiatives. Recognize and reward employees who contribute to enhancing workflows and driving efficiency. Cultivating a culture that values continuous improvement empowers employees to actively seek opportunities to optimize software workflows and processes.

By implementing these strategies, organizations can optimize their software workflows and processes, leading to increased efficiency, reduced costs, improved quality, and enhanced overall productivity. Continuous evaluation, collaboration, and a focus on innovation ensure that workflows evolve and adapt to the changing needs of the organization, resulting in sustained improvements in efficiency and performance.

Integrating Software with Existing Systems

Integrating software with existing systems is a critical aspect of maximizing efficiency and productivity within an organization. Chapter 4 of "The Art of Business Software: A Comprehensive Guide for Success" explores the strategies and best practices for integrating software with existing systems. In this section, we delve into the key considerations and approaches for successful software integration.

Assess Existing Systems and Infrastructure

Begin by assessing your organization's existing systems and infrastructure. Identify the various systems, applications, and databases that are currently in use. Understand how these systems function and interact with each other. Evaluate the compatibility and integration capabilities of these systems with the new software to identify any potential challenges or opportunities.

Define Integration Goals and Objectives

Clearly define your integration goals and objectives. Determine what you aim to achieve through integration, such as streamlining data exchange, eliminating manual data entry, or creating a centralized view of information. Setting clear objectives ensures that the integration efforts align with your organization's strategic priorities and desired outcomes.

Select the Right Integration Approach

Choose the most appropriate integration approach based on your organization's needs, capabilities, and the systems being integrated. Common integration approaches include application programming interfaces (APIs), data connectors, middleware platforms, and custom integration solutions. Assess the pros and cons of each approach and select the one that best fits your integration requirements.

Engage IT and Software Vendor Expertise

Collaborate with your internal IT team and the software vendor to leverage their expertise and guidance throughout the integration process. Engage in open communication and establish a partnership to ensure a smooth integration. Leverage their knowledge of the software's integration capabilities and seek their advice on best practices, potential challenges, and mitigation strategies.

Map Data and Process Flows

Map out the data and process flows between the existing systems and the software being integrated. Identify the data elements that need to be exchanged, shared, or synchronized between systems. Understand how different processes within your organization interact with the integrated software and define the optimal data and process flows.

Ensure Data Integrity and Consistency

Pay close attention to data integrity and consistency during the integration process. Implement data validation and cleansing mechanisms to ensure that data is accurate, complete, and consistent across systems. Define data mapping and transformation rules to ensure that data is properly interpreted and utilized by the integrated software.

Plan and Execute Integration Testing

Develop a comprehensive integration testing plan to validate the integration solution. Test various scenarios and use cases to ensure seamless data exchange, proper functionality, and system compatibility. Conduct both unit testing (testing individual components) and end-to-end testing (testing the integrated system as a whole) to identify and resolve any integration issues or anomalies.

Establish Monitoring and Error Handling Mechanisms

Implement monitoring mechanisms to track the performance and reliability of the integrated systems. Set up alerts and notifications to proactively identify any integration errors or failures. Establish error handling processes and define escalation paths to quickly address and resolve integration-related issues.

Ensure Security and Compliance

Prioritize security and compliance considerations during integration. Implement appropriate security measures to protect data during transit and storage. Ensure that the integrated systems adhere to regulatory requirements and industry standards. Conduct regular security audits and assessments to identify and mitigate any potential vulnerabilities.

Provide Training and Support

Offer training and support to users and stakeholders involved in the integrated systems. Ensure that they understand how the integration works, how to access integrated data, and how to utilize the integrated features effectively. Provide ongoing support channels to address any integration-related questions or issues that may arise.

By following these best practices, organizations can successfully integrate software with existing systems, enabling seamless data exchange, streamlining processes, and improving overall efficiency. Integration allows organizations to leverage the capabilities of different systems, create a unified view of information, and eliminate silos, leading to enhanced decision-making and improved operational effectiveness.

Monitoring and Measuring Software Performance

Monitoring and measuring software performance is essential to ensure optimal functionality, identify areas for improvement, and maximize efficiency. Chapter 4 of "The Art of Business Software: A Comprehensive Guide for Success" explores the strategies and best practices for monitoring and measuring software performance. In this section, we delve into key considerations and approaches to effectively monitor and measure software performance.

Establish Key Performance Indicators (KPIs)

Define relevant Key Performance Indicators (KPIs) that align with your organization's goals and objectives. These KPIs may include metrics such as response time, system availability, error rates, user adoption rates, or task completion time. Establishing KPIs provides a benchmark for evaluating software performance and identifying areas that require attention.

Use Performance Monitoring Tools

Leverage performance monitoring tools that provide real-time insights into the software's performance. These tools can track key metrics, generate performance reports, and send alerts or notifications when issues or anomalies are detected. Select monitoring tools that are compatible with your software and can provide granular visibility into system performance.

Monitor System Availability and Response Time

Track the availability and response time of the software to ensure it meets desired service level agreements (SLAs) and user expectations. Monitor system uptime and response times for different tasks or functions. This allows you to identify any performance bottlenecks or areas where improvements can be made to enhance user experience and overall efficiency.

Monitor User Adoption and Engagement

Measure user adoption and engagement to gauge the effectiveness of the software. Monitor metrics such as user logins, active users, feature usage, or user feedback. This helps identify areas where additional training or support may be needed to improve user adoption and maximize the software's value.

Conduct User Experience Testing

Regularly conduct user experience testing to assess the software's usability and user satisfaction. Gather feedback from end-users through surveys, interviews, or user experience testing sessions. This feedback provides insights into how the software can be improved to better meet user needs, streamline processes, and enhance overall efficiency.

Analyze Performance Data

Analyze the collected performance data to identify patterns, trends, or anomalies. Look for areas where performance may be suboptimal, such as slow response times, frequent errors, or inefficient workflows. Use data analysis techniques to uncover root causes and make data-driven decisions for optimizing software performance.

Conduct Load and Stress Testing

Perform load and stress testing to evaluate how the software performs under heavy workloads or peak usage periods. Simulate scenarios that represent real-world conditions to assess the software's scalability, stability, and performance limits. This testing helps identify potential performance bottlenecks and allows you to optimize system resources and configurations accordingly.

Regularly Review and Update Performance Goals

Regularly review and update performance goals based on changing business requirements and technological advancements.

Periodically assess the relevance of existing KPIs and consider incorporating new metrics that align with emerging needs or trends. This ensures that the performance measurement aligns with organizational objectives and enables effective performance management.

Continuously Optimize and Improve Performance

Use the insights gathered from performance monitoring to identify areas for improvement and optimization. Implement enhancements, updates, or configurations that address performance bottlenecks or align with industry best practices. Continuously optimize the software to ensure that it operates at its peak performance and supports organizational efficiency.

Foster a Culture of Continuous Improvement

Promote a culture of continuous improvement within the organization. Encourage stakeholders to actively participate in performance monitoring, analysis, and improvement initiatives. Foster a collaborative environment where feedback is valued, and performance optimization is seen as a shared responsibility. This culture of continuous improvement drives ongoing enhancements to software performance and overall organizational efficiency.

By following these best practices, organizations can effectively monitor and measure software performance, enabling them to proactively identify and address performance issues, optimize workflows, and continuously improve operational efficiency. Regular performance monitoring and analysis help organizations stay aligned with their goals, deliver a positive user experience, and maximize the value derived from their software investments.

Chapter 5
Security and Data Protection

Chapter 5 of "The Art of Business Software: A Comprehensive Guide for Success" focuses on security and data protection. In today's digital landscape, safeguarding sensitive information and ensuring the integrity of data are paramount for organizations. This chapter explores the strategies and best practices for maintaining robust security measures and protecting valuable data assets.

The chapter begins by emphasizing the importance of establishing a comprehensive security framework. It highlights the need for organizations to develop a security policy that outlines security objectives, roles and responsibilities, and the procedures for protecting data and software assets. A well-defined security framework provides a roadmap for implementing effective security controls and mitigating risks.

Next, the chapter delves into the critical aspects of access control and user management. It explores strategies for managing user access privileges, implementing strong authentication mechanisms, and enforcing the principle of least privilege. By properly managing user access, organizations can reduce the risk of unauthorized data breaches and ensure that sensitive information is accessible only to authorized individuals.

The chapter then discusses the significance of data encryption and encryption protocols. It explains the importance of encrypting data at rest and in transit to protect it from unauthorized access. The chapter explores different encryption methods, such as symmetric and asymmetric encryption, and highlights the role of encryption protocols in securing data transmissions. Implementing robust encryption measures helps safeguard data confidentiality and integrity.

Furthermore, the chapter explores the importance of regular data backups and disaster recovery planning. It emphasizes the need for organizations to establish backup procedures, schedule regular backups, and test data restoration processes. By maintaining up-to-date backups and implementing disaster recovery strategies, organizations can mitigate the impact of data loss or system failures and ensure business continuity.

The chapter also addresses the importance of vulnerability management and patch management. It highlights the need for organizations to stay informed about software vulnerabilities, apply security patches promptly, and conduct regular vulnerability assessments. By proactively managing vulnerabilities, organizations can reduce the risk of cyberattacks and maintain a secure software environment.

Moreover, the chapter discusses the significance of user awareness and training in maintaining security. It emphasizes the need to educate users about security best practices, such as password hygiene, phishing awareness, and social engineering prevention. By fostering a culture of security awareness and providing ongoing training, organizations can empower users to play an active role in safeguarding data and software assets.

The chapter concludes by discussing compliance with relevant regulations and standards. It emphasizes the need for organizations to understand and comply with applicable data protection and privacy regulations, industry-specific standards, and legal requirements. Compliance helps protect customer data, maintain trust, and mitigate the risk of legal and reputational consequences.

In summary, Chapter 5 provides readers with a comprehensive understanding of security and data protection in the context of business software. By establishing a robust security framework, implementing access controls, encrypting data, maintaining backups, managing vulnerabilities, promoting user awareness, and ensuring compliance, organizations can proactively protect their valuable data assets, mitigate risks, and maintain a secure software environment.

Importance of Cybersecurity in Business Software

In today's digital landscape, cybersecurity plays a crucial role in protecting organizations from cyber threats and ensuring the integrity, confidentiality, and availability of their data and software assets. Business software, being an integral part of organizational operations, must be equipped with robust cybersecurity measures. This section explores the importance of cybersecurity in business software and the reasons why organizations should prioritize it.

Protection against Data Breaches

Data breaches can have severe consequences, including financial losses, damage to reputation, and legal and regulatory penalties. Business software often stores and processes sensitive information, such as customer data, intellectual property, and financial records. Robust cybersecurity measures in business software help safeguard this information, reducing the risk of data breaches and protecting both the organization and its stakeholders.

Safeguarding Intellectual Property

Many businesses rely on intellectual property as a core asset, including trade secrets, proprietary algorithms, or confidential business strategies. Cybersecurity measures in business software protect these valuable assets from unauthorized access, theft, or exploitation. By securing the software that manages and stores intellectual property, organizations can maintain their competitive advantage and safeguard their innovations.

Mitigating Financial Losses

Cybersecurity incidents can lead to significant financial losses for organizations. Cyberattacks can result in financial fraud, ransom demands, or disruptions to business operations, leading to revenue loss and increased costs for incident response and recovery. Strong cybersecurity measures in business software help mitigate these financial risks by reducing the likelihood and impact of successful cyberattacks.

Preserving Customer Trust

Customer trust is vital for the success of any organization. When customers entrust their data to a business, they expect it to be handled securely and responsibly. Demonstrating a commitment to cybersecurity by implementing robust measures in business software helps preserve customer trust. It assures customers that their sensitive information is protected, fostering long-term relationships and maintaining a positive brand image.

Ensuring Regulatory Compliance

Organizations are subject to various data protection and privacy regulations, such as the General Data Protection Regulation (GDPR) or the California Consumer Privacy Act (CCPA). Business software must comply with these regulations to avoid legal consequences and reputational damage. By implementing cybersecurity measures, organizations demonstrate their commitment to data protection and fulfill their compliance obligations.

Preventing Disruptions to Operations

Cybersecurity incidents can lead to disruptions in business operations, ranging from network downtime to the loss of critical data. Business software is often an essential component of day-to-day operations, and any compromise to its security can hinder productivity and cause operational delays. Robust cybersecurity measures ensure the continuity and smooth functioning of business software, minimizing disruptions and maintaining operational efficiency.

Protecting Against Advanced Threats

Cyber threats are continuously evolving, with sophisticated attacks becoming more prevalent. Business software must stay ahead of these threats by implementing advanced cybersecurity measures. This includes intrusion detection and prevention systems, real-time threat intelligence, and proactive vulnerability management. By integrating these security capabilities into business software, organizations can effectively defend against advanced threats.

Preserving Brand Reputation

A cybersecurity incident can severely damage an organization's brand reputation. Negative publicity surrounding a data breach or cyberattack can erode customer trust and deter potential customers from engaging with the organization. Prioritizing cybersecurity in business software helps safeguard the brand reputation by demonstrating a commitment to protecting sensitive information and maintaining a secure environment for stakeholders.

In summary, cybersecurity in business software is of paramount importance to protect against data breaches, safeguard intellectual property, mitigate financial losses, preserve customer trust, ensure regulatory compliance, prevent disruptions to operations, defend against advanced threats, and preserve brand reputation. By prioritizing cybersecurity measures in their software, organizations can create a strong security posture and safeguard their critical assets in today's increasingly digital and interconnected world.

Implementing Data Protection Measures

Implementing robust data protection measures is crucial to safeguard sensitive information and maintain the integrity of data within an organization. Chapter 5 of "The Art of Business Software: A Comprehensive Guide for Success" focuses on data protection and security. In this section, we explore key considerations and best practices for implementing effective data protection measures.

Data Classification

Start by classifying your data based on its sensitivity and importance. Categorize data into different levels of sensitivity, such as public, internal, confidential, and highly sensitive. This classification helps determine the appropriate level of protection required for each category and guides the implementation of data protection measures.

Access Control and User Permissions

Implement strong access control mechanisms to restrict access to sensitive data. Enforce the principle of least privilege, granting access rights based on job roles and responsibilities. Regularly review and update user permissions to ensure that access is granted on a need-to-know basis. Implement multi-factor authentication for an added layer of security when accessing sensitive data.

Encryption

Utilize encryption techniques to protect data at rest and in transit. Encrypt sensitive data using strong encryption algorithms and ensure that encryption keys are securely managed. This includes encrypting data stored in databases, file systems, and backups, as well as data transmitted over networks or stored on portable devices. Encryption provides an additional layer of protection, even if unauthorized access occurs.

Data Loss Prevention

Implement data loss prevention (DLP) measures to prevent accidental or intentional data leaks. Use DLP software or solutions that can detect and prevent the unauthorized transfer, storage, or sharing of sensitive data. Configure DLP rules to monitor and block sensitive data based on predefined policies, helping to prevent data breaches and maintain data confidentiality.

Regular Data Backups

Establish a robust data backup strategy to ensure data availability and resilience. Regularly back up critical data using reliable backup solutions. Consider a combination of onsite and offsite backups to safeguard against physical damage or disasters. Test data restoration procedures periodically to verify the integrity and accessibility of backup data.

Secure Data Storage

Implement secure data storage practices to protect data from unauthorized access or theft. Use secure storage solutions, such as encrypted databases or file systems, to store sensitive information. Regularly patch and update storage systems to address security vulnerabilities. Implement strong access controls and monitoring mechanisms to ensure that only authorized individuals can access and modify stored data.

Data Retention and Disposal

Establish data retention policies to determine the appropriate duration for storing data. Regularly review and dispose of data that is no longer necessary or required by legal or regulatory obligations. Use secure data destruction methods when disposing of storage media to prevent data recovery. By implementing proper data retention and disposal practices, organizations can minimize the risk of data exposure.

Security Awareness and Training

Promote security awareness among employees through comprehensive training programs. Educate employees about data protection best practices, such as password hygiene, phishing prevention, and safe data handling. Reinforce the importance of data protection and create a culture of security awareness within the organization. Regularly communicate security updates and emerging threats to keep employees informed and vigilant.

Incident Response and Reporting

Establish an incident response plan to handle data breaches or security incidents effectively. Define roles, responsibilities, and escalation procedures to ensure a coordinated response. Implement mechanisms to detect, report, and respond to security incidents promptly. Regularly conduct incident response drills and simulations to test the effectiveness of the plan and identify areas for improvement.

Regular Security Audits and Assessments

Conduct regular security audits and assessments to evaluate the effectiveness of data protection measures. Perform vulnerability assessments, penetration testing, and security audits to identify and address potential weaknesses. Stay informed about evolving security threats and apply security patches and updates promptly. Regular audits and assessments help ensure that data protection measures remain robust and effective.

By implementing these data protection measures, organizations can strengthen their security posture and safeguard sensitive information. Effective data protection not only protects the organization from data breaches and compliance violations but also enhances customer trust and confidence in the organization's commitment to data security.

Handling User Access and Permissions

Properly managing user access and permissions is a critical aspect of maintaining data security and ensuring that sensitive information remains protected within an organization. Chapter 5 of "The Art of Business Software: A Comprehensive Guide for Success" addresses the importance of handling user access and permissions. In this section, we explore key considerations and best practices for managing user access effectively.

Role-Based Access Control (RBAC)

Implement a role-based access control (RBAC) model to manage user access and permissions. RBAC assigns user permissions based on predefined roles and responsibilities within the organization. Define roles that reflect job functions and access needs, and assign appropriate permissions to each role. This approach ensures that users have access only to the data and functionalities necessary for their roles, reducing the risk of unauthorized access.

Principle of Least Privilege (PoLP)

Adhere to the principle of least privilege (PoLP) when granting user permissions. Grant users the minimum level of access required to perform their job functions effectively. Avoid giving excessive permissions that go beyond what is necessary for their roles. Regularly review and update user permissions as job responsibilities change to ensure permissions align with the principle of least privilege.

User Provisioning and De-Provisioning

Establish clear processes for user provisioning and de-provisioning. When onboarding new employees or granting access to new users, follow a standardized process to assign appropriate roles and permissions. Similarly, when an employee leaves the organization or changes roles, promptly remove or adjust their permissions. Effective user provisioning and de-provisioning minimize the risk of unauthorized access by ensuring that permissions are granted and revoked in a timely manner.

Two-Factor Authentication (2FA)

Implement two-factor authentication (2FA) to enhance user authentication and access security. 2FA requires users to provide an additional authentication factor, such as a temporary code sent to their mobile device, in addition to their username and password. This adds an extra layer of protection against unauthorized access, even if login credentials are compromised.

Regular Access Reviews

Conduct regular access reviews to ensure that user permissions remain appropriate and up to date. Periodically review user access rights and permissions, comparing them against job roles and responsibilities. Identify any discrepancies or unnecessary permissions and promptly make adjustments. Regular access reviews help maintain the integrity of access control and minimize the risk of unauthorized access.

Segregation of Duties

Implement segregation of duties (SoD) to prevent conflicts of interest and reduce the risk of fraud. Segregate duties in a way that requires multiple individuals to complete critical tasks or processes. This ensures that no single user has complete control or access to sensitive functions or data. SoD helps mitigate the risk of malicious activities or unintentional errors that can result from excessive access privileges.

Access Logging and Monitoring

Implement logging and monitoring mechanisms to track user activities and detect any suspicious or unauthorized access attempts. Maintain logs of user access, login attempts, and critical system activities. Regularly monitor these logs to identify any abnormal patterns or potential security incidents. Promptly investigate and take appropriate actions if any unauthorized access is detected.

User Awareness and Training

Educate users about their role in maintaining data security and the importance of responsible access management. Provide training on best practices for password security, recognizing phishing attempts, and adhering to data protection policies. Promote a culture of security awareness among users, ensuring that they understand their responsibilities in safeguarding sensitive information.

Implement Access Controls within Software

Utilize access control features provided by the business software itself. Leverage built-in capabilities to enforce user permissions, configure role-based access, and control data visibility within the software. Ensure that the access controls align with your organization's security policies and requirements.

Regular Security Audits and Assessments

Conduct regular security audits and assessments to evaluate the effectiveness of user access and permissions. Perform periodic reviews of user permissions, access logs, and user provisioning processes. Identify and address any gaps or vulnerabilities in access control. Regular audits and assessments help ensure that user access and permissions align with the organization's security policies and remain secure over time.

By implementing these best practices for handling user access and permissions, organizations can maintain strong data security, reduce the risk of unauthorized access, and protect sensitive information from potential breaches or unauthorized disclosure. Effective access management ensures that users have appropriate access to data and functionalities while maintaining the confidentiality, integrity, and availability of organizational resources.

Ensuring Compliance with Privacy Regulations

Compliance with privacy regulations is essential for organizations to protect individual privacy rights, maintain trust, and mitigate the risk of legal and reputational consequences. Chapter 5 of "The Art of Business Software: A Comprehensive Guide for Success" highlights the importance of ensuring compliance with privacy regulations. In this section, we explore key considerations and best practices for achieving compliance with privacy regulations.

Understand Applicable Privacy Regulations

Thoroughly research and understand the privacy regulations that apply to your organization's operations and the data it handles. Common regulations include the General Data Protection Regulation (GDPR), California Consumer Privacy Act (CCPA), and Health Insurance Portability and Accountability Act (HIPAA). Familiarize yourself with the specific requirements, obligations, and principles outlined in these regulations.

Conduct Privacy Impact Assessments

Perform privacy impact assessments (PIAs) to identify and evaluate the potential privacy risks associated with your business processes, software applications, and data handling practices. Assess how personal data is collected, stored, processed, and shared within your organization. Identify any privacy vulnerabilities or gaps that may exist and develop strategies to address them effectively.

Implement Data Protection Policies and Procedures

Develop and implement comprehensive data protection policies and procedures that align with the requirements of privacy regulations. These policies should outline how personal data is handled, including data collection, storage, retention, processing, and sharing practices. Ensure that employees are aware of and trained on these policies to promote consistent adherence to privacy guidelines.

Obtain Proper Consent

Obtain appropriate consent from individuals when collecting and processing their personal data. Ensure that the consent obtained is freely given, specific, informed, and unambiguous. Clearly communicate the purposes for which the data will be used and any third parties with whom it may be shared. Provide individuals with the option to withdraw consent and explain the implications of doing so.

Implement Data Minimization and Retention Practices

Adopt data minimization principles by collecting and retaining only the personal data necessary to fulfill specific purposes. Regularly review and update data retention practices to ensure compliance with privacy regulations. Establish clear guidelines for data retention periods, deletion, or anonymization to limit the storage of personal data beyond what is necessary.

Secure Personal Data

Implement appropriate security measures to protect personal data from unauthorized access, disclosure, alteration, or destruction. Employ encryption, access controls, firewalls, and other security technologies to safeguard personal data. Regularly assess the effectiveness of security measures through audits and penetration testing, and promptly address any identified vulnerabilities or weaknesses.

Provide Data Subject Rights

Facilitate the exercise of data subject rights as mandated by privacy regulations. Establish procedures for individuals to access, rectify, restrict processing, and delete their personal data. Respond promptly to data subject requests and ensure that the necessary mechanisms are in place to fulfill these requests within the specified time frames.

Establish Data Breach Response Procedures

Develop clear and comprehensive procedures for responding to and reporting data breaches. Establish incident response teams, define roles and responsibilities, and document the steps to be taken in the event of a data breach. Ensure that data breach notifications are sent to affected individuals, regulatory authorities, and other relevant parties as required by privacy regulations.

Regularly Train and Educate Employees

Educate employees on the importance of privacy regulations, their roles and responsibilities in ensuring compliance, and the implications of non-compliance. Provide regular training and awareness programs that cover data protection, privacy principles, and best practices for handling personal data. Foster a culture of privacy awareness throughout the organization.

Conduct Privacy Audits and Assessments

Periodically conduct privacy audits and assessments to evaluate compliance with privacy regulations. Assess the effectiveness of data protection measures, policies, and procedures. Identify any areas of non-compliance or potential privacy risks and take appropriate remedial actions.

By diligently ensuring compliance with privacy regulations, organizations can protect individual privacy rights, maintain customer trust, and demonstrate their commitment to responsible data handling. Adhering to privacy regulations not only helps organizations avoid legal and reputational risks but also promotes transparency, accountability, and ethical business practices in the digital age.

Chapter 6
Maintaining and Upgrading Business Software

Chapter 6 of "The Art of Business Software: A Comprehensive Guide for Success" focuses on the critical aspects of maintaining and upgrading business software. In this chapter, we explore the importance of software maintenance, the benefits of regular updates and upgrades, and best practices for effectively managing software maintenance and upgrades.

The chapter begins by highlighting the significance of software maintenance. Software maintenance involves activities such as bug fixes, performance optimizations, security patches, and compatibility updates. Regular maintenance ensures that the software remains stable, secure, and reliable over time. It helps address software issues, improve functionality, and enhance the user experience.

Next, the chapter discusses the benefits of keeping software up to date through regular updates and upgrades. Updates typically involve incremental improvements, bug fixes, and minor feature enhancements, while upgrades introduce significant changes, new features, or architectural improvements. Staying current with software updates and upgrades offers advantages such as improved security, enhanced functionality, increased efficiency, and access to the latest technologies.

The chapter then explores best practices for managing software maintenance and upgrades effectively. It emphasizes the importance of establishing a structured maintenance process that includes regular monitoring, issue tracking, and prioritization of maintenance tasks. Implementing change management practices helps ensure that updates and upgrades are planned, tested, and deployed efficiently, minimizing disruption to business operations.

Furthermore, the chapter emphasizes the significance of a comprehensive testing strategy. Thoroughly test software updates and upgrades in a controlled environment to identify any compatibility issues, functional regressions, or performance impacts. This includes unit testing, integration testing, and user acceptance testing to validate the stability and compatibility of the software with existing systems and workflows.

The chapter also stresses the importance of maintaining documentation throughout the software lifecycle. Documentation should include release notes, user guides, and version control information. It facilitates effective communication with stakeholders, provides guidance on new features and changes, and ensures that users have the necessary information to adapt to updates and upgrades seamlessly.

Additionally, the chapter emphasizes the importance of user training and support. Communicate software changes and new features to users through training programs, knowledge-sharing sessions, or online resources. Provide adequate support channels, such as help desks or user communities, to address user queries and issues related to software updates or upgrades. This promotes user adoption, minimizes resistance to change, and maximizes the value derived from software improvements.

The chapter concludes by emphasizing the need for continuous monitoring and evaluation. Regularly assess the effectiveness of software updates and upgrades by monitoring performance, user feedback, and key performance indicators (KPIs). Gather insights from users, analyze software usage patterns, and identify opportunities for further optimization or enhancements.

In summary, Chapter 6 highlights the importance of maintaining and upgrading business software. By effectively managing software maintenance, staying up to date with updates and upgrades, implementing rigorous testing, providing documentation and user support, and continuously evaluating software performance, organizations can ensure that their software remains robust, secure, and aligned with evolving business needs.

Establishing a Software Maintenance Plan

A well-defined software maintenance plan is essential for organizations to effectively manage and ensure the long-term stability, performance, and reliability of their business software. This section highlights key considerations and best practices for establishing a comprehensive software maintenance plan.

Identify Maintenance Objectives

Begin by identifying the objectives of your software maintenance plan. Consider factors such as bug fixing, security updates, performance optimizations, compatibility improvements, and feature enhancements. Clearly define the goals and priorities of maintenance activities to align them with organizational objectives and user needs.

Define Maintenance Processes and Procedures

Develop structured processes and procedures for managing software maintenance. Outline the steps involved in identifying, prioritizing, and resolving maintenance tasks. Establish mechanisms for issue tracking, reporting, and resolution. Define roles and responsibilities within the maintenance process to ensure clear ownership and accountability.

Establish Maintenance Prioritization Criteria

Establish criteria for prioritizing maintenance tasks based on factors such as severity, impact on business operations, and user feedback. Categorize maintenance tasks into different priority levels to guide resource allocation and ensure critical issues are addressed promptly. This prioritization framework helps optimize maintenance efforts and focus resources on the most impactful tasks.

Implement Change Management Practices

Adopt change management practices to ensure that software updates and maintenance activities are properly planned, tested, and deployed. Establish a change management process that includes change requests, impact assessments, change approvals, and rollback plans. Adhering to change management practices minimizes risks and disruption to business operations during maintenance activities.

Establish Testing and Quality Assurance Procedures

Include thorough testing and quality assurance procedures as part of your software maintenance plan. Develop a comprehensive testing strategy that covers functional testing, regression testing, and performance testing. Test software updates and fixes in a controlled environment to ensure compatibility, stability, and quality. Implement automated testing tools and frameworks to streamline the testing process.

Implement Version Control and Documentation

Utilize version control systems to manage software releases and track changes. Maintain clear documentation of software versions, release notes, and known issues. Document the purpose and impact of each software update or maintenance task. This documentation helps stakeholders understand the changes and enables effective communication during the maintenance process.

Provide User Support and Communication

Establish channels for user support and communication regarding software maintenance. Communicate maintenance schedules, updates, and known issues to users in a timely manner. Provide clear instructions and documentation on how users can report issues or seek assistance. Maintain open lines of communication with users to address their concerns, provide training, and gather feedback on software performance.

Establish Monitoring and Evaluation Mechanisms

Implement monitoring and evaluation mechanisms to assess the effectiveness of maintenance activities. Define key performance indicators (KPIs) and metrics to measure software performance, user satisfaction, and the impact of maintenance efforts. Regularly review these metrics, gather user feedback, and conduct post-maintenance evaluations to identify areas for improvement and optimization.

Plan for Future Enhancements

Consider future enhancements and feature updates as part of the software maintenance plan. Engage with stakeholders, gather user feedback, and align maintenance efforts with evolving business needs. Continuously evaluate market trends, technological advancements, and user expectations to identify opportunities for adding value and improving the software's capabilities over time.

Continuously Improve the Maintenance Process

Regularly assess the effectiveness of the software maintenance plan and seek opportunities for improvement. Gather feedback from stakeholders, including users, development teams, and IT personnel, to identify pain points and areas for optimization. Incorporate lessons learned from past maintenance activities into the plan to enhance future maintenance processes and outcomes.

By implementing these best practices and establishing a comprehensive software maintenance plan, organizations can ensure that their business software remains reliable, secure, and aligned with evolving needs. Effective maintenance practices minimize downtime, enhance user satisfaction, and contribute to the long-term success of the software application.

Performing Regular Updates and Patches

Regular updates and patches are critical for maintaining the security, stability, and performance of business software. This section outlines the importance of performing regular updates and patches and highlights best practices for effectively managing these processes.

Importance of Regular Updates and Patches

Regular updates and patches are essential for addressing vulnerabilities, bugs, and security risks identified in the software. These updates may include bug fixes, performance improvements, compatibility enhancements, and new features. By keeping the software up to date, organizations can protect against emerging threats, ensure compatibility with evolving technologies, and optimize the user experience.

Establish an Update and Patch Management Process

Establish a systematic process for managing updates and patches. Define roles and responsibilities for individuals involved in the update and patch management, including development teams, IT personnel, and stakeholders. Develop guidelines and procedures to ensure updates are deployed in a controlled manner and minimize disruption to business operations.

Stay Informed About Updates and Patches

Stay informed about the availability of updates and patches for the business software. Monitor official software channels, vendor websites, security bulletins, and mailing lists to receive notifications about new releases. Subscribe to relevant industry publications and security news sources to stay updated on emerging vulnerabilities and security patches.

Prioritize Updates and Patches

Prioritize updates and patches based on their criticality and impact on the software's functionality and security. Evaluate the severity of vulnerabilities or bugs addressed by each update and patch. Consider factors such as the potential for data breaches, system instability, or compliance risks. Focus on high-priority updates first to address critical security vulnerabilities promptly.

Test Updates and Patches

Before deploying updates and patches to production environments, thoroughly test them in a controlled testing environment. This includes functional testing, regression testing, and performance testing to ensure that the updates do not introduce new issues or adversely affect the software's performance. Develop a comprehensive testing plan and use automated testing tools to streamline the testing process.

Plan and Schedule Updates and Patches

Develop a well-defined plan and schedule for deploying updates and patches. Consider factors such as the availability of maintenance windows, business operation priorities, and potential user impact. Notify relevant stakeholders in advance about scheduled updates to minimize disruption. Establish rollback procedures to mitigate any unforeseen issues during the update deployment.

Implement Change Management Practices

Integrate updates and patches into the organization's change management practices. Create a change request process to document and track updates and patches. Conduct impact assessments to evaluate the potential effects on existing systems, integrations, or workflows. Seek appropriate approvals for deploying updates and patches, ensuring adherence to change management protocols.

Maintain Backup and Recovery Strategies

Before applying updates and patches, ensure that proper backup and recovery strategies are in place. Perform regular backups of critical data and system configurations. Test data restoration procedures to ensure that data can be recovered in case of any unforeseen issues during the update or patch deployment process.

Communicate Updates and Patches to Users

Effectively communicate updates and patches to users, providing clear information about the changes, bug fixes, and new features. Inform users about any potential disruptions or system downtime during the update process. Provide instructions and support channels for users to report issues or seek assistance related to the updates or patches.

Monitor and Evaluate the Update Process

Regularly monitor and evaluate the effectiveness of the update and patch management process. Track metrics such as update deployment success rate, time to deploy updates, and user satisfaction post-update. Gather user feedback and address any reported issues promptly. Continuously improve the update process based on lessons learned and user input.

By following these best practices, organizations can ensure that regular updates and patches are performed effectively and efficiently. Regularly updating the business software helps maintain its security, performance, and functionality, enabling organizations to stay ahead of potential threats and provide a reliable and secure software environment.

Evaluating the Need for Software Upgrades

Evaluating the need for software upgrades is a crucial step in maintaining an efficient and competitive technology infrastructure. This section discusses the importance of assessing the need for software upgrades and provides guidance on effective evaluation practices.

Business Requirements and Objectives

Start by aligning software upgrades with the organization's business requirements and objectives. Evaluate whether the current software version adequately supports the evolving needs of the organization. Consider factors such as scalability, performance, security, compatibility with other systems, and the ability to meet regulatory requirements. Assess if an upgrade is necessary to address these needs and drive business growth.

Security Vulnerabilities and Patching

One of the primary reasons for software upgrades is to address security vulnerabilities. Regularly assess the security posture of the current software version. Stay informed about any reported vulnerabilities and the availability of security patches. Evaluate the severity and potential impact of these vulnerabilities on the organization's systems and data. Determine if an upgrade is essential to address critical security concerns.

Feature Enhancements and Functionality

Evaluate the availability of new features and functionalities in the upgraded software version. Consider whether these enhancements align with the organization's business objectives and can provide a competitive advantage. Assess if the new features would improve productivity, streamline processes, enhance user experience, or enable integration with other systems. Determine if the benefits offered by the upgraded software justify the investment and effort required for the upgrade.

End-of-Life and Support

Check if the current software version has reached its end-of-life (EOL) or will soon be unsupported by the vendor. Unsupported software may lack essential security updates, bug fixes, and technical support, leaving the organization exposed to risks. Evaluate the implications of using an unsupported version and consider the need for an upgrade to ensure ongoing vendor support, access to maintenance services, and compliance with industry standards.

Cost-Benefit Analysis

Perform a cost-benefit analysis to evaluate the financial impact of the software upgrade. Consider the costs associated with the upgrade, such as licensing fees, migration expenses, training, and potential system downtime during the transition. Compare these costs with the anticipated benefits, such as increased productivity, reduced maintenance efforts, improved security, and enhanced functionality. Assess whether the expected benefits outweigh the investment required for the upgrade.

System Performance and Scalability

Evaluate the current system performance and scalability limitations. Assess if the existing software version can effectively handle the growing demands of the organization. Consider factors such as data volume, user concurrency, response times, and resource utilization. Determine if an upgrade is necessary to enhance system performance, optimize resource usage, and accommodate future growth.

User Feedback and Satisfaction

Gather feedback from end-users regarding their experiences with the current software version. Identify pain points, usability issues, or functionality gaps that may be addressed in the upgraded version. Evaluate user satisfaction levels and determine if an upgrade would improve user experience, productivity, and overall satisfaction.

Industry Trends and Technological Advancements

Stay informed about industry trends and technological advancements relevant to the software domain. Assess if the current software version aligns with emerging technologies and industry best practices. Consider if an upgrade would enable the organization to leverage new technologies, such as cloud computing, artificial intelligence, or data analytics, to gain a competitive edge.

Evaluate the ROI

Determine the return on investment (ROI) associated with the software upgrade. Assess the potential cost savings, increased productivity, revenue growth, or competitive advantages that may result from the upgrade. Evaluate the projected timeframe for achieving ROI and weigh it against the organization's financial and strategic goals.

Consult with Stakeholders and Experts

Engage with relevant stakeholders, including IT teams, business units, and key users, to gather their input and insights regarding the need for software upgrades. Seek advice from industry experts, consultants, or vendor representatives who can provide valuable guidance based on their domain expertise and experience.

By evaluating the need for software upgrades using these considerations, organizations can make informed decisions that align with their business objectives, security requirements, user satisfaction, and financial considerations. An effective evaluation process ensures that software upgrades are undertaken with a clear understanding of the potential benefits and impacts on the organization's technology landscape.

Managing Software Licenses and Support Contracts

Effective management of software licenses and support contracts is crucial for organizations to ensure compliance, optimize costs, and maintain uninterrupted access to critical software resources. This section outlines best practices for managing software licenses and support contracts.

License Inventory and Documentation

Maintain an up-to-date inventory of all software licenses used within the organization. Document the details of each license, including vendor information, license keys, terms and conditions, and the number of authorized users or installations. Centralize this information in a license management system or database to ensure easy accessibility and accurate tracking.

Compliance and License Audits

Regularly review and assess software license compliance to ensure adherence to the terms and conditions of each license agreement. Conduct periodic license audits to verify that the organization is using software within the authorized scope. Identify any instances of non-compliance and take appropriate actions to rectify them, such as obtaining additional licenses or adjusting software usage.

License Optimization and Cost Control

Optimize software license usage to minimize costs and maximize the value derived from each license. Conduct a thorough analysis of license utilization across the organization to identify any underutilized or unused licenses. Consider implementing license management tools or solutions that provide insights into usage patterns and enable license reallocation or consolidation. Negotiate volume discounts or explore alternative licensing models to optimize costs.

Renewal and Expiration Management

Establish a proactive approach to manage software license renewals and expirations. Maintain a calendar or system to track renewal dates and deadlines. Start the renewal process well in advance to ensure uninterrupted access to software resources. Monitor support contract expirations to avoid any lapses in technical support, updates, or access to vendor resources.

Vendor Relationship Management

Nurture positive relationships with software vendors to enhance support and license management. Establish regular communication channels with vendor representatives to stay updated on licensing changes, upgrades, and product roadmaps. Leverage these relationships to negotiate favorable licensing terms, obtain discounts, and address any licensing or support-related issues promptly.

Contract Negotiation and Review

Thoroughly review software license agreements and support contracts before entering into them. Ensure a clear understanding of licensing terms, usage rights, support levels, and any associated costs. Identify any clauses related to usage restrictions, maintenance fees, or termination conditions that may impact the organization. If necessary, involve legal or procurement teams to review and negotiate contracts to align with the organization's interests.

Maintenance and Support Performance Tracking

Monitor the performance of support contracts to ensure that vendors fulfill their obligations effectively. Track response times, issue resolution rates, and overall satisfaction with vendor support services. Address any service level agreement (SLA) deviations promptly and communicate concerns or expectations to the vendor. Maintain documentation of support interactions and issue resolutions for future reference.

Software Lifecycle Planning

Develop a software lifecycle plan that aligns with the organization's technology strategy and objectives. Consider factors such as end-of-life announcements, product roadmaps, and the availability of software updates or upgrades. Plan for software migrations or replacements when products reach their end-of-life stage or when more suitable alternatives become available.

Centralize License and Support Information

Centralize license and support contract information in a dedicated repository or contract management system. Ensure that key stakeholders have access to this repository to facilitate easy retrieval of license details, contract terms, and renewal information. Maintain backups of critical license and support documentation to safeguard against data loss or system failures.

Regular Review and Auditing

Conduct regular reviews of software license usage, support contract terms, and vendor performance. Evaluate the effectiveness of license management processes and identify areas for improvement. Perform periodic audits to verify compliance and ensure that license management practices align with organizational policies and regulatory requirements.

By implementing these best practices, organizations can effectively manage software licenses and support contracts, minimize compliance risks, optimize costs, and maintain uninterrupted access to critical software resources. Proactive license management and strong vendor relationships contribute to a robust software ecosystem that supports business operations and drives organizational success.

Chapter 7
Managing Business Software Projects

Chapter 7 of "The Art of Business Software: A Comprehensive Guide for Success" delves into the essential aspects of managing business software projects. This chapter explores key considerations, methodologies, and best practices for effectively managing software projects within an organization.

The chapter begins by emphasizing the importance of project planning. It highlights the significance of defining project objectives, scope, deliverables, and timelines. A well-defined project plan serves as a roadmap, guiding the project team through various stages of the software development lifecycle. It helps align project goals with organizational objectives and sets clear expectations for project stakeholders.

Next, the chapter explores different project management methodologies, such as waterfall, agile, and hybrid approaches. It provides insights into the strengths and weaknesses of each methodology, allowing project managers to choose the most suitable approach based on project requirements, team dynamics, and organizational culture. It emphasizes the need for flexibility and adaptability in project management methodologies to accommodate evolving project needs.

The chapter then discusses the key activities involved in managing business software projects, including requirements gathering, resource allocation, task scheduling, and risk management. It emphasizes the significance of effective communication, collaboration, and stakeholder engagement throughout the project lifecycle. Project managers are encouraged to establish clear lines of communication, foster team collaboration, and actively involve stakeholders to ensure project success.

Furthermore, the chapter highlights the importance of project monitoring and control. It emphasizes the need for regular progress tracking, status reporting, and issue management. Project managers should establish key performance indicators (KPIs) and metrics to measure project progress, quality, and adherence to timelines. By monitoring project performance, project managers can identify deviations from the plan and take corrective actions in a timely manner.

The chapter also addresses the critical aspect of managing project risks. It emphasizes the need for proactive risk identification, analysis, and mitigation strategies. Project managers should develop risk management plans and establish contingency measures to address potential risks that could impact project timelines, budgets, or deliverables. By identifying and mitigating risks early on, project managers can minimize the impact of unforeseen events on the project's overall success.

Additionally, the chapter discusses the significance of change management in software projects. It emphasizes the need for a structured change management process to handle changes in project requirements, scope, or priorities. Project managers should ensure that change requests are thoroughly evaluated, communicated, and implemented in a controlled manner, minimizing disruptions to the project's progress.

The chapter concludes by emphasizing the importance of continuous improvement and learning from project experiences. Project managers should conduct post-project reviews to assess successes, challenges, and lessons learned. They should identify areas for improvement and document best practices for future projects. By incorporating feedback and insights from previous projects, organizations can enhance their project management practices and increase the chances of successful software project outcomes.

In summary, Chapter 7 provides valuable guidance for managing business software projects effectively. By following the principles and best practices outlined in this chapter, project managers can navigate the complexities of software projects, deliver successful outcomes, and contribute to the overall success of their organizations.

Project Management Principles for Software Implementation

Implementing software projects requires effective project management principles to ensure successful outcomes. This section highlights key project management principles specifically tailored for software implementation projects.

Define Clear Project Objectives and Scope

Clearly define the project objectives, scope, and deliverables. Document the desired outcomes and ensure alignment with organizational goals. Establish a shared understanding among project stakeholders about the project's purpose, benefits, and boundaries. This clarity sets the foundation for effective project planning and execution.

Adopt an Appropriate Project Management Methodology

Select a project management methodology that suits the nature of the software implementation project. Agile methodologies, such as Scrum or Kanban, are commonly used for software projects due to their flexibility and iterative approach. Waterfall methodologies can be suitable for projects with well-defined requirements and sequential phases. Consider hybrid approaches that combine the strengths of different methodologies to best fit project needs.

Involve Key Stakeholders from the Beginning

Engage key stakeholders from the project's outset, including end-users, management, IT personnel, and subject matter experts. Involve them in requirement gathering, solution design, and decision-making processes. Their insights and involvement ensure that the software solution aligns with their needs, increases user adoption, and enhances project success.

Develop a Detailed Project Plan

Create a comprehensive project plan that outlines the activities, milestones, timelines, and resource allocations. Break down the project into manageable tasks, estimate effort and dependencies, and establish realistic timelines. Ensure that the project plan accounts for contingencies and addresses potential risks. Regularly review and update the plan as the project progresses.

Establish Effective Communication Channels

Implement clear and open lines of communication among project team members and stakeholders. Establish regular communication channels, such as meetings, progress reports, and collaboration tools, to ensure efficient information flow. Encourage active and transparent communication to address concerns, resolve issues, and keep all stakeholders informed about project progress.

Manage Requirements and Scope Changes

Develop a robust requirements management process to handle changes in project requirements and scope. Establish a change control mechanism to evaluate, approve, and track changes. Clearly communicate the impact of changes on the project's timeline, budget, and deliverables. Balancing the need for flexibility with proper change management helps prevent scope creep and maintain project focus.

Mitigate Risks and Anticipate Challenges

Identify project risks and proactively develop risk management strategies. Conduct a thorough risk assessment to identify potential issues that could impact project success. Develop risk response plans and establish mitigation measures to address identified risks. Regularly monitor and reassess risks throughout the project's lifecycle.

Foster Collaboration and Empower the Project Team

Promote a collaborative and empowering environment for the project team. Encourage open communication, knowledge sharing, and teamwork. Empower team members to make decisions, take ownership of their tasks, and contribute to project success. Recognize and appreciate their efforts to foster motivation and commitment.

Conduct Regular Quality Assurance and Testing

Implement a robust quality assurance and testing process to ensure that the software solution meets the defined requirements and quality standards. Develop comprehensive test plans, execute thorough testing, and address identified issues promptly. Regularly assess the software's performance, functionality, and usability to deliver a high-quality product.

Monitor Progress and Adapt as Needed

Monitor project progress against the established plan and key performance indicators (KPIs). Use project management tools and techniques to track milestones, budgets, and resource utilization. Identify deviations early on and take corrective actions promptly. Maintain flexibility to adapt to changing circumstances while keeping the project on track.

By adhering to these project management principles, organizations can effectively manage software implementation projects and increase the likelihood of achieving successful outcomes. The principles emphasize proper planning, stakeholder engagement, effective communication, risk management, and continuous monitoring to ensure the smooth and successful delivery of the software solution.

Creating a Project Plan and Defining Milestones

Creating a well-structured project plan with defined milestones is crucial for effectively managing software implementation projects. This section outlines the key steps involved in creating a project plan and establishing meaningful milestones.

Understand Project Objectives and Scope

Start by gaining a clear understanding of the project objectives and scope. Collaborate with key stakeholders to identify the desired outcomes, deliverables, and constraints. Document the project's purpose, goals, and specific requirements to serve as the foundation for the project plan.

Break the Project into Phases

Divide the project into logical phases or stages based on the project methodology and specific requirements. Each phase should represent a major step towards achieving the project objectives. Common phases may include requirements gathering, solution design, development, testing, deployment, and post-implementation support.

Define Milestones

Identify significant milestones that represent key achievements or completion points within each project phase. Milestones act as checkpoints for measuring progress and providing clear indications of project advancement. They should be specific, measurable, and tied to deliverables or key project events. Examples of milestones include completing requirements documentation, finishing system testing, or obtaining user acceptance.

Establish Milestone Dependencies and Sequencing

Determine the relationships and dependencies between milestones. Identify milestones that must be completed before others can start or progress. Sequence the milestones in a logical order to ensure a smooth flow of project activities. Consider any constraints or dependencies on resources, external factors, or dependencies on prior project phases.

Assign Resources and Define Responsibilities

Identify the project team members, their roles, and responsibilities for each milestone. Assign project tasks and deliverables to team members based on their expertise and availability. Clearly communicate expectations, deadlines, and dependencies to ensure everyone understands their roles and contributes effectively to milestone achievement.

Estimate Effort and Duration

Estimate the effort and duration required for each milestone based on the project scope, complexity, and available resources. Collaborate with team members to gather input and insights for accurate estimations. Consider dependencies, risks, and potential challenges that may impact the time needed to complete each milestone.

Establish Timeline and Schedule

Create a project timeline that outlines the start and end dates for each milestone. Ensure that the project schedule accounts for dependencies, resource availability, and realistic timeframes. Allocate sufficient time for testing, review cycles, and any unforeseen delays that may arise during the project execution.

Develop a Communication Plan

Define a communication plan that outlines how project progress, milestone achievements, and any changes will be communicated to stakeholders. Identify the frequency, channels, and recipients of project updates and status reports. Establish a clear escalation path for addressing issues, risks, or changes that may impact milestone delivery.

Continuously Monitor and Review Progress

Regularly monitor project progress against the established timeline and milestones. Use project management tools and techniques to track actual progress, identify any deviations, and take corrective actions when necessary. Conduct regular project reviews and status meetings to ensure alignment and make informed decisions based on project performance.

Adjust and Refine the Project Plan

As the project progresses, be prepared to adjust and refine the project plan and milestones based on new insights, changing requirements, or unforeseen circumstances. Continuously evaluate project risks, scope changes, and stakeholder feedback to ensure the project plan remains realistic and aligned with the evolving needs of the organization.

By following these steps, project managers can create a comprehensive project plan with well-defined milestones that serve as critical guideposts throughout the software implementation project. The project plan provides a roadmap for the project team, ensures effective resource allocation, facilitates communication, and enables stakeholders to track progress and measure project success.

Tracking Progress and Managing Risks

Tracking progress and effectively managing risks are essential aspects of software implementation projects. This section outlines best practices for tracking progress and managing risks throughout the project lifecycle.

Tracking ProgressDefine:Key Performance Indicators (KPIs)

Establish specific KPIs to measure project progress. KPIs can include milestones achieved, tasks completed, budget utilization, resource allocation, and quality metrics. Clearly define the metrics and measurement criteria for each KPI to ensure accurate tracking and reporting.

Implement Project Management Tools

Utilize project management tools to track and monitor project progress. These tools can help visualize project timelines, track tasks and dependencies, assign resources, and provide real-time updates. Choose tools that align with the project management methodology being used and ensure they are accessible to all relevant team members.

Regularly Review and Update the Project Schedule

Continuously review and update the project schedule to reflect the current status of tasks and milestones. Identify any delays or bottlenecks and take appropriate actions to address them. Keep the schedule visible and communicate any changes to stakeholders in a timely manner.

Conduct Progress Meetings

Hold regular progress meetings with the project team to discuss task updates, address challenges, and ensure alignment. Use these meetings to track progress against milestones, review completed tasks, and identify any issues or risks that may affect project timelines. Encourage open communication and collaboration to maintain a transparent and accountable project environment.

Monitor Resource Utilization

Regularly monitor resource utilization to ensure that team members are allocated efficiently and effectively. Identify any resource constraints or imbalances and take corrective actions to optimize resource allocation. This includes managing workload, addressing skill gaps, and considering the need for additional resources when necessary.

Managing Risks: Identify and Assess Risks

Conduct a comprehensive risk assessment at the beginning of the project to identify potential risks and their potential impact on project success. Involve key stakeholders and project team members in the risk identification process. Assess the probability and severity of each risk and prioritize them based on their potential impact.

Develop a Risk Response Plan

Develop a risk response plan that outlines strategies for mitigating, accepting, transferring, or avoiding identified risks. Assign responsibilities for risk mitigation actions and establish clear escalation paths for reporting and addressing risks. Continuously monitor and update the risk response plan as new risks emerge or existing risks evolve.

Implement Risk Monitoring and Control

Regularly monitor identified risks throughout the project lifecycle. Track the status of risk mitigation actions and assess the effectiveness of risk control measures. Maintain open communication channels to encourage the reporting of new risks or changes in the severity of existing risks. Proactively address risks to prevent them from becoming major project issues.

Communicate and Engage Stakeholders

Keep stakeholders informed about identified risks, their potential impacts, and the actions being taken to address them. Provide regular risk status updates in project reports and meetings. Engage stakeholders in risk discussions and decision-making processes to ensure their buy-in and involvement in risk management efforts.

Conduct Contingency Planning

Develop contingency plans for high-impact risks that have the potential to significantly disrupt the project. Identify alternative approaches, backup options, or fallback strategies to mitigate the consequences of such risks. Ensure that contingency plans are well-documented, communicated to relevant stakeholders, and activated when needed.

Foster a Culture of Risk Awareness

Promote a culture of risk awareness and proactive risk management within the project team. Encourage team members to identify and report risks promptly, share lessons learned, and propose risk mitigation strategies. By fostering a collaborative and risk-aware environment, the project team can collectively contribute to effective risk management.

By effectively tracking progress and managing risks throughout the software implementation project, project managers can maintain project momentum, proactively address challenges, and increase the likelihood of project success. Regular progress tracking and risk management activities help keep the project on track, mitigate potential issues, and ensure that the project is delivered within the defined scope, timelines, and quality standards.

Communicating Effectively with Stakeholders

Effective communication with stakeholders is crucial for the success of software implementation projects. Clear and transparent communication fosters collaboration, builds trust, manages expectations, and ensures alignment among project participants. This section outlines best practices for communicating effectively with stakeholders throughout the project lifecycle.

Identify Key Stakeholders

Identify the stakeholders who have an interest or influence in the project. This includes project sponsors, end-users, management, executives, team members, and external parties. Understand their roles, expectations, and communication preferences to tailor your communication strategies accordingly.

Establish Communication Channels

Determine the most appropriate communication channels for different stakeholders and project needs. This may include face-to-face meetings, emails, project management software, collaboration tools, video conferences, and progress reports. Utilize a combination of channels to ensure effective and timely information flow.

Tailor Messages to the Audience

Adapt your communication style and language to suit the needs and understanding of different stakeholders. Avoid technical jargon when communicating with non-technical stakeholders, and provide sufficient context and explanations for complex concepts. Tailoring messages ensures that stakeholders comprehend and engage with the information effectively.

Set Clear Communication Objectives

Define the objectives for each communication interaction. Whether it is providing updates, seeking feedback, addressing concerns, or making decisions, clarity in communication objectives helps focus conversations and ensures stakeholders understand the purpose and desired outcomes of the communication.

Use Active Listening

Practice active listening when engaging with stakeholders. Pay attention to their perspectives, concerns, and feedback. Encourage stakeholders to share their thoughts and actively seek their input. By demonstrating active listening, you promote a culture of open dialogue and foster stakeholder engagement.

Provide Regular Project Updates

Maintain a regular cadence of project updates to keep stakeholders informed about project progress, milestones achieved, and any changes or challenges. Consider providing a combination of written reports, presentations, and meetings to cater to different stakeholders' communication preferences. Ensure updates are concise, relevant, and tailored to the stakeholders' needs.

Be Transparent and Honest

Promote transparency by sharing accurate and honest information about the project's status, challenges, and risks. Address issues and concerns promptly and openly. Transparency builds trust and confidence among stakeholders, enabling effective collaboration and problem-solving.

Manage Expectations

Set realistic expectations by clearly communicating project constraints, limitations, and potential risks upfront. Clearly articulate project timelines, deliverables, and any anticipated deviations from the original plan. Regularly update stakeholders on any changes to project scope, timeline, or requirements to manage expectations effectively.

Seek and Incorporate Feedback

Actively seek feedback from stakeholders at various project stages. Encourage stakeholders to provide input, suggestions, and concerns related to project deliverables, processes, or outcomes. Incorporate valuable feedback into decision-making and project adjustments to ensure stakeholder satisfaction and engagement.

Document and Archive Communications

Maintain records of project communications, decisions, and agreements. Document meeting minutes, action items, and important correspondence to create a comprehensive project history. This documentation serves as a reference for future discussions, ensures accountability, and assists in resolving conflicts or addressing disputes.

Tailor Communication to Project Phases

Adapt your communication strategies and frequency based on the project phase. In the initial stages, focus on providing comprehensive project overviews and eliciting stakeholder requirements. During execution, emphasize progress updates and issue resolution. In the closing phase, communicate project outcomes, lessons learned, and next steps.

Celebrate Successes and Recognize Contributions

Acknowledge and celebrate project milestones, achievements, and the contributions of stakeholders. Publicly recognize team members and stakeholders for their efforts and successes. This fosters a positive project environment and motivates stakeholders to continue their commitment and engagement.

By following these best practices, project managers can establish effective communication with stakeholders, maintain stakeholder engagement, and ensure a shared understanding of project objectives, progress, and outcomes. Effective communication contributes to stronger stakeholder relationships, increased project support, and ultimately, successful software implementation.

Chapter 8
Future Trends in Business Software

Chapter 8 of "The Art of Business Software: A Comprehensive Guide for Success" explores emerging trends and future developments in the field of business software. This chapter provides insights into the evolving landscape of technology and its potential impact on businesses. It highlights key trends that are expected to shape the future of business software.

Artificial Intelligence and Machine Learning

Artificial intelligence (AI) and machine learning (ML) are revolutionizing business software. AI-powered applications can automate repetitive tasks, analyze vast amounts of data, and provide intelligent insights. ML algorithms enable software to learn and adapt, improving decision-making processes, customer experiences, and operational efficiency. The chapter explores the potential applications of AI and ML in various business domains and their role in shaping the future of software.

Cloud Computing and Software as a Service (SaaS)

Cloud computing and the rise of Software as a Service (SaaS) have transformed the way businesses access and utilize software solutions. The chapter discusses the benefits of cloud-based software, such as scalability, flexibility, and cost-effectiveness. It explores the growing adoption of cloud-based business software, the shift from on-premises deployments to cloud-based solutions, and the implications for businesses in terms of data security, integration, and vendor management.

Internet of Things (IoT:

The Internet of Things (IoT) is a rapidly expanding network of interconnected devices that collect and exchange data. The chapter explores how IoT technology integrates with business software, enabling real-time monitoring, data analysis, and automation. It discusses the potential impact of IoT on industries such as manufacturing, logistics, healthcare, and smart cities, as well as the opportunities and challenges associated with IoT integration.

Blockchain Technology

Blockchain technology, known for its secure and transparent nature, has the potential to revolutionize various aspects of business software. The chapter explores how blockchain can enhance trust, security, and efficiency in areas such as supply chain management, financial transactions, and data privacy. It discusses the emergence of blockchain-based platforms, smart contracts, and decentralized applications, and their implications for future business software solutions.

Enhanced Data Analytics and Business Intelligence

Advancements in data analytics and business intelligence are transforming how businesses leverage data for insights and decision-making. The chapter discusses the integration of advanced analytics tools, predictive modeling, and data visualization techniques into business software. It highlights the importance of data-driven decision-making, the emergence of self-service analytics, and the integration of analytics capabilities directly within software applications.

User Experience and Design Thinking

The focus on user experience (UX) and design thinking is increasingly shaping the development of business software. The chapter explores how businesses are prioritizing intuitive interfaces, streamlined workflows, and personalized experiences for end-users. It discusses the role of design thinking methodologies in creating software that meets user needs, enhances productivity, and fosters user adoption and satisfaction.

Cybersecurity and Privacy

As business software becomes more interconnected and data-driven, the need for robust cybersecurity and data privacy measures becomes paramount. The chapter explores the growing importance of cybersecurity in business software, including data encryption, threat detection, and access controls. It also examines the evolving landscape of privacy regulations and the impact on the design and implementation of business software.

Throughout the chapter, case studies, industry examples, and expert insights are utilized to provide a comprehensive understanding of these future trends. The chapter concludes by highlighting the importance of staying updated on emerging technologies, understanding their implications, and adapting business strategies to leverage the potential of these trends.

By exploring these future trends, businesses can gain insights into the evolving landscape of business software and proactively position themselves to harness the benefits of these advancements. This knowledge empowers businesses to make informed decisions, embrace innovation, and stay ahead in a rapidly changing technological landscape.

Emerging Technologies and Their Impact on Business Software

Emerging technologies have a profound impact on the development and capabilities of business software. This section explores some of the key emerging technologies and their potential implications for business software.

Artificial Intelligence (AI) and Machine Learning (ML)

AI and ML technologies are revolutionizing business software by enabling automation, predictive analytics, and intelligent decision-making. AI-powered software applications can automate repetitive tasks, analyze vast amounts of data, and provide valuable insights. ML algorithms enable software to learn from data and improve performance over time. The integration of AI and ML into business software enhances efficiency, personalization, and data-driven decision-making.

Internet of Things (IoT)

The Internet of Things (IoT) is a network of interconnected devices embedded with sensors, software, and connectivity, allowing them to collect and exchange data. IoT technology has the potential to revolutionize business software by enabling real-time data monitoring, remote device management, and automation. Businesses can leverage IoT data to optimize operations, enhance customer experiences, and drive innovation across industries.

Blockchain Technology

Blockchain technology offers secure and transparent decentralized transactional systems. It has the potential to transform various aspects of business software, including supply chain management, financial transactions, and data security. Blockchain provides a tamper-proof and auditable record of transactions, improving trust, traceability, and efficiency in business processes. Incorporating blockchain into business software can enhance data integrity, streamline transactions, and reduce fraud.

Cloud Computing and Software as a Service (SaaS)

Cloud computing and the rise of Software as a Service (SaaS) have transformed the way businesses access and utilize software solutions. Cloud-based business software offers scalability, flexibility, and cost-effectiveness by leveraging remote servers and infrastructure. SaaS models enable businesses to access software applications on-demand, reducing the need for on-premises installations and maintenance. Cloud computing and SaaS facilitate collaboration, data sharing, and remote work, driving efficiency and agility in business operations.

Enhanced Data Analytics and Business Intelligence

Advancements in data analytics and business intelligence are empowering businesses to gain valuable insights from their data. Business software incorporates advanced analytics tools, predictive modeling, and data visualization techniques to enable data-driven decision-making. These technologies facilitate in-depth analysis of large datasets, identification of patterns and trends, and actionable insights. Enhanced data analytics and business intelligence capabilities empower businesses to optimize processes, improve customer experiences, and gain a competitive edge.

Augmented Reality (AR) and Virtual Reality (VR)

AR and VR technologies are finding applications in business software, particularly in areas such as training, simulation, and visualization. AR enhances real-world experiences by overlaying digital information onto the physical environment, while VR immerses users in virtual environments. Businesses can leverage AR and VR in areas like product design, virtual meetings, and training simulations, improving collaboration, engagement, and productivity.

Natural Language Processing (NLP) and Voice Recognition

NLP and voice recognition technologies enable business software to understand and process human language, opening new avenues for human-computer interaction. Chatbots, virtual assistants, and voice-enabled interfaces are becoming prevalent in business software, facilitating natural and intuitive user interactions. These technologies enhance customer support, automate routine tasks, and improve user experiences.

These emerging technologies have the potential to reshape business software, enabling businesses to streamline processes, enhance decision-making, and drive innovation. Organizations that embrace and adapt to these technologies can gain a competitive advantage, deliver better products and services, and transform the way they operate in an increasingly digital world.

Predictive Analytics and Artificial Intelligence (AI)

Predictive analytics and AI are transformative technologies that have a significant impact on business software. This section explores the concepts of predictive analytics and AI and their implications for business software applications.

Predictive Analytics

Predictive analytics involves the use of historical data, statistical algorithms, and machine learning techniques to forecast future outcomes or behaviors. By analyzing patterns and trends in data, predictive analytics enables businesses to make informed predictions and proactive decisions. In the context of business software, predictive analytics algorithms can uncover valuable insights, anticipate customer preferences, optimize processes, and mitigate risks.

Applications of Predictive Analytics in Business Software: Sales and Marketing

Predictive analytics can help businesses identify potential customers, personalize marketing campaigns, forecast sales, and optimize pricing strategies. By analyzing customer data, purchase history, and market trends, business software can provide actionable insights for targeted marketing efforts and improved sales forecasting.

Risk Management

Predictive analytics algorithms can assess risks by analyzing historical data and identifying patterns that precede adverse events. This enables businesses to predict and mitigate risks, such as fraud, financial losses, or operational disruptions. Risk management software powered by predictive analytics can provide real-time risk assessments, alerts, and recommendations.

Supply Chain Optimization

Predictive analytics can optimize supply chain operations by analyzing demand patterns, forecasting inventory needs, and identifying potential bottlenecks or disruptions. Business software with predictive analytics capabilities can enable proactive inventory management, efficient logistics planning, and improved supplier collaboration.

Artificial Intelligence (AI)

AI refers to the simulation of human intelligence in machines that can perform tasks that typically require human intelligence, such as understanding natural language, recognizing patterns, and making informed decisions. AI technologies, such as machine learning, natural language processing, and computer vision, enable software applications to learn from data, adapt to new information, and automate complex tasks.

Applications of AI in Business Software:

Intelligent Automation: AI enables business software to automate routine and repetitive tasks, improving efficiency and productivity. Intelligent automation can streamline processes, such as data entry, document processing, and customer support, reducing manual effort and human errors.

Natural Language Processing (NLP)

NLP allows business software to understand and interpret human language, facilitating conversational interfaces, chatbots, and voice-enabled interactions. NLP-powered applications can analyze customer inquiries, provide personalized responses, and enhance user experiences.

Decision Support Systems

AI-based decision support systems provide recommendations and insights to support decision-making processes. By analyzing vast amounts of data, AI-powered business software can identify patterns, detect anomalies, and generate predictive models that assist in strategic decision-making.

Customer Experience Enhancement

AI technologies enable businesses to personalize customer experiences by analyzing customer data, preferences, and behavior. AI-powered recommendation engines can suggest relevant products or services, personalize marketing messages, and optimize user interfaces to enhance customer satisfaction and engagement.

The integration of predictive analytics and AI into business software empowers organizations to leverage data-driven insights, automate processes, optimize decision-making, and enhance customer experiences. By embracing these technologies, businesses can gain a competitive edge, improve operational efficiency, and unlock new opportunities for growth and innovation.

Cloud-based software solutions have transformed the way businesses access, deploy, and utilize software applications. This section explores the concept of cloud computing and its implications for businesses using cloud-based software solutions.

Cloud Computing

Cloud computing refers to the delivery of computing services over the internet, allowing users to access and use software applications, storage, and computing resources remotely. Rather than relying on local servers or infrastructure, cloud-based software leverages remote servers hosted by third-party providers. Users can access the software through web browsers or dedicated applications, with data and processing handled on the provider's servers.

Key Implications of Cloud-Based Software Solutions for Businesses: Scalability and Flexibility

Cloud-based software solutions offer scalability, allowing businesses to adjust their resource usage based on demand. As business needs grow or change, cloud-based software can easily scale up or down, providing the required computing power, storage, and user access. This flexibility enables businesses to align their software resources with their evolving needs, avoiding the constraints of traditional on-premises software deployments.

Cost-effectiveness

Cloud-based software solutions offer cost advantages over traditional on-premises software. Instead of investing in costly hardware, maintenance, and software licenses, businesses can access cloud-based software through a subscription model or pay-as-you-go pricing. This reduces upfront costs and allows businesses to optimize their software expenses based on actual usage. Cloud-based software also eliminates the need for on-site infrastructure, reducing maintenance and upgrade costs.

Accessibility and Collaboration

Cloud-based software can be accessed from anywhere with an internet connection, enabling remote work and enhancing collaboration. Employees can access the software and collaborate in real-time, regardless of their physical location. This accessibility promotes flexibility, productivity, and efficient collaboration among geographically dispersed teams, contractors, and stakeholders.

Automatic Updates and Maintenance

Cloud-based software providers are responsible for maintaining and updating the software infrastructure. Businesses no longer need to worry about manually installing updates or managing software patches. Cloud-based software is automatically updated by the provider, ensuring businesses have access to the latest features, bug fixes, and security enhancements without additional effort.

Data Security and Backup

Cloud-based software solutions prioritize data security and offer robust backup mechanisms. Cloud providers implement stringent security measures, such as data encryption, access controls, and regular security audits, to protect sensitive business data. Additionally, cloud-based software often includes data backup and disaster recovery features, ensuring business continuity and data resilience in the event of a system failure or data loss.

Integration and Ecosystems

Cloud-based software solutions often provide integration capabilities with other software applications and services through APIs (Application Programming Interfaces). This enables businesses to connect their cloud-based software with other systems, such as customer relationship management (CRM), accounting, or e-commerce platforms. Integration capabilities foster seamless data flow, process automation, and streamlined workflows across different software solutions.

Rapid Deployment and Time-to-Value

Cloud-based software solutions enable rapid deployment, allowing businesses to start using the software quickly. With minimal infrastructure setup and configuration required, businesses can reduce the time between software acquisition and achieving value from the software. This agility supports faster adoption, quicker time-to-market, and accelerated business processes.

By leveraging cloud-based software solutions, businesses can access a wide range of software applications, enhance collaboration, optimize costs, and focus on their core competencies. Cloud computing offers scalability, flexibility, cost-effectiveness, and seamless software updates, enabling businesses to adapt to changing market needs and gain a competitive edge in today's dynamic business environment.

Mobile applications play a significant role in enhancing the functionality and accessibility of business software. This section explores the role of mobile applications in business software and their implications for businesses.

Enhanced Accessibility and Mobility

Mobile applications allow users to access business software and critical data from anywhere, at any time. Users can conveniently access software functionalities, view real-time information, and perform tasks while on the go, using their smartphones or tablets. Mobile apps enable employees to stay connected and productive, even when they are away from their desks or traveling. This accessibility enhances productivity, responsiveness, and agility in business operations.

Improved User Experience and Engagement

Mobile applications are designed with a focus on user experience, providing intuitive interfaces and optimized workflows for mobile devices. By tailoring software functionalities and user interfaces specifically for mobile platforms, business software can offer a seamless and user-friendly experience. This improves user engagement, adoption, and satisfaction, as mobile apps cater to the preferences and habits of mobile device users.

Real-time Data and Notifications

Mobile applications enable real-time access to business data, enabling users to receive up-to-date information and timely notifications. This real-time data availability empowers users to make informed decisions, respond quickly to business situations, and stay updated on critical events. Mobile apps can provide push notifications, alerts, and reminders, ensuring that users are promptly informed of important updates or tasks.

On-the-Go Productivity and Collaboration

Mobile applications facilitate on-the-go productivity and collaboration among team members. Users can access and update documents, participate in discussions, and collaborate with colleagues through mobile apps. Mobile-enabled collaboration features enhance communication, coordination, and teamwork, even when team members are geographically dispersed or working remotely.

Location-based Services and Contextual Information

Mobile applications can leverage location-based services and contextual information to enhance the functionality of business software. By utilizing GPS or beacon technology, mobile apps can provide location-specific information, targeted recommendations, or personalized experiences. For example, field service management software can optimize routes based on real-time location data, improving efficiency and customer service.

Integration with Device Features

Mobile applications can seamlessly integrate with various device features, such as cameras, microphones, and sensors. This integration allows users to capture images, scan barcodes, record audio, or utilize biometric authentication within the business software. Leveraging device features enhances data input accuracy, simplifies processes, and enriches the functionality of business software.

Offline Capabilities

Mobile applications can offer offline capabilities, allowing users to work and access data even when an internet connection is temporarily unavailable. Offline mode enables users to continue their tasks, sync data once connectivity is restored, and ensure uninterrupted productivity. This is particularly beneficial for field service workers, sales representatives, or employees in remote areas with limited network coverage.

Personalization and User Preferences

Mobile applications can provide personalized experiences by adapting to user preferences, settings, and usage patterns. Mobile apps can remember user preferences, provide customized recommendations, and offer tailored content based on user behavior. This personalization enhances user engagement, efficiency, and satisfaction with the business software.

By incorporating mobile applications into business software strategies, organizations can leverage the power of mobility, real-time data, and enhanced user experiences. Mobile apps empower employees to be productive, collaborate effectively, and make informed decisions, regardless of their location. The role of mobile applications in business software aligns with the growing need for flexibility, accessibility, and mobile-centric workflows in today's digital business landscape.

In conclusion, "The Art of Business Software: A Comprehensive Guide for Success" provides a comprehensive exploration of the world of business software and its applications. The book covers various aspects of business software, including its importance in the modern digital landscape, planning and selecting the right software, implementing and maximizing its efficiency, ensuring security and data protection, maintaining and upgrading software, managing software projects, and the future trends shaping the industry.

The importance of business software in the modern digital landscape cannot be overstated. It has become an essential tool for businesses of all sizes, enabling them to streamline operations, enhance productivity, and gain a competitive edge. From managing finances and customer relationships to optimizing workflows and analyzing data, business software plays a pivotal role in driving growth and success.

Throughout the book, readers gain valuable insights into the various aspects of business software, supported by real-world examples, case studies, and expert advice. The book emphasizes the need for careful planning and selection of software solutions that align with business needs and goals. It provides guidance on the implementation process, addressing key considerations such as change management, user training, and successful adoption.

The book also highlights the significance of maximizing the efficiency of business software. It explores topics such as customizing software to meet specific business needs, optimizing workflows and processes, integrating software with existing systems, and monitoring software performance. By focusing on these aspects, businesses can extract the maximum value from their software investments and drive operational excellence.

Security and data protection are critical concerns in the digital era, and the book addresses these topics extensively. It emphasizes the need to implement robust measures to safeguard sensitive data, handle user access and permissions, and ensure compliance with privacy regulations. By prioritizing security and data protection, businesses can maintain trust, protect valuable information, and mitigate the risks associated with cyber threats.

"The Art of Business Software" also delves into the importance of maintaining and upgrading software to keep up with evolving business needs and technological advancements. It guides readers on establishing maintenance plans, performing updates and patches, evaluating the need for upgrades, and managing software licenses and support contracts. These practices ensure the long-term sustainability and relevance of business software solutions.

Furthermore, the book provides valuable insights into managing business software projects, emphasizing the importance of project management principles, creating project plans, defining milestones, and effectively communicating with stakeholders. By following best practices in project management, businesses can enhance collaboration, manage risks, and successfully deliver software projects on time and within budget.

Lastly, the book looks towards the future, exploring emerging trends in business software such as artificial intelligence, cloud computing, IoT, and blockchain technology. It highlights the potential impact of these trends on businesses and encourages readers to stay informed and embrace innovation to stay ahead in a rapidly evolving technological landscape.

"The Art of Business Software: A Comprehensive Guide for Success" serves as a valuable resource for businesses and professionals seeking to navigate the complex world of business software. Whether it is selecting the right software solution, implementing it effectively, ensuring security and efficiency, or staying abreast of future trends, this book provides the necessary knowledge and insights to succeed in harnessing the power of business software for growth and prosperity.

Throughout "The Art of Business Software: A Comprehensive Guide for Success," several key points have been discussed to provide readers with a comprehensive understanding of business software. Here is a recap of the key points covered in the book:

Importance of Business Software

Business software plays a crucial role in the modern digital landscape, enabling businesses to streamline operations, enhance productivity, and gain a competitive edge.

Planning and Selecting Software

Careful planning and selection of software solutions are essential for aligning software with business needs and goals. This involves assessing business requirements, conducting feasibility studies, evaluating different options, and making informed decisions.

Implementing Software

Successful implementation of business software requires thorough preparation, including creating implementation strategies, defining milestones, managing change, and ensuring user training and adoption.

Maximizing Software Efficiency

Customizing and configuring software, optimizing workflows and processes, integrating with existing systems, and monitoring performance are key strategies for maximizing the efficiency and value of business software.

Security and Data Protection

Protecting sensitive data, implementing data protection measures, managing user access and permissions, and ensuring compliance with privacy regulations are crucial for maintaining data security and privacy.

Maintaining and Upgrading Software

Establishing maintenance plans, performing regular updates and patches, evaluating the need for upgrades, and managing software licenses and support contracts are important for the long-term sustainability and relevance of business software.

Managing Software Projects

Applying project management principles, creating project plans, tracking progress, managing risks, and effectively communicating with stakeholders are vital for successful software project management.

Future Trends

Exploring emerging technologies such as artificial intelligence, cloud computing, IoT, and blockchain, and understanding their potential impact on business software, allows businesses to stay ahead and adapt to future trends.

These key points collectively provide readers with a comprehensive guide to navigate the world of business software, empowering them to make informed decisions, optimize efficiency, enhance security, and leverage emerging technologies for growth and success.

"The Art of Successful Business Software Implementation and Management" serves as a comprehensive guide for businesses looking to navigate the complex process of implementing and managing software effectively. By emphasizing key principles, strategies, and best practices, this book provides valuable insights to help businesses achieve success in their software initiatives.

Successful business software implementation and management require careful planning, alignment with business goals, and a focus on user adoption. This book highlights the importance of assessing business needs, conducting feasibility studies, and selecting software solutions that align with organizational requirements. It emphasizes the need for effective communication, user training, and change management to ensure smooth adoption and maximize the benefits of software implementation.

The book underscores the significance of maximizing software efficiency through customization, workflow optimization, and integration with existing systems. By continuously monitoring and measuring software performance, businesses can identify areas for improvement and proactively optimize their software solutions.

Security and data protection are critical aspects of successful software management. The book stresses the importance of implementing robust security measures, handling user access and permissions, and ensuring compliance with privacy regulations. By prioritizing security, businesses can protect valuable data, maintain trust, and mitigate the risks associated with cyber threats.

Additionally, the book highlights the need for ongoing software maintenance, regular updates, and evaluation of upgrade needs. It emphasizes the importance of managing software licenses and support contracts to ensure continuous functionality and access to technical support.

Successful software implementation and management also require effective project management practices. The book emphasizes the significance of project planning, defining milestones, tracking progress, managing risks, and engaging stakeholders throughout the project lifecycle. By following project management principles, businesses can enhance collaboration, manage expectations, and deliver software projects successfully.

Finally, the book explores emerging trends in the industry, such as artificial intelligence, cloud computing, IoT, and blockchain. By keeping abreast of these trends, businesses can proactively adapt and leverage emerging technologies to stay competitive and drive innovation.

In conclusion, "The Art of Successful Business Software Implementation and Management" offers a comprehensive and practical guide for businesses seeking success in their software initiatives. By focusing on key principles, strategies, and best practices, businesses can navigate the complex landscape of software implementation and management with confidence, leading to improved operational efficiency, enhanced productivity, and sustainable growth.

Conclusion:

"The Art of Successful Business Software Implementation and Management" serves as a comprehensive and invaluable guide for businesses navigating the complex world of software implementation and management. Through a careful examination of key principles, strategies, and best practices, this book equips businesses with the knowledge and tools necessary to achieve success in their software initiatives.

One of the fundamental lessons highlighted in this book is the importance of aligning software initiatives with overarching business goals. Understanding the specific needs and requirements of the organization is crucial for selecting the right software solutions. By conducting thorough assessments and feasibility studies, businesses can identify software options that best fit their unique circumstances. Additionally, the book emphasizes the significance of effective communication and collaboration among stakeholders, ensuring that all parties are aligned and invested in the success of the software implementation.

Successful software implementation goes beyond the initial deployment phase; it requires a focus on user adoption and change management. By prioritizing user training and providing ongoing support, businesses can facilitate the transition to new software systems and encourage employees to fully embrace the new tools. The book emphasizes the need for a well-defined change management strategy that addresses potential resistance and ensures a smooth transition. Ultimately, successful adoption of business software relies on creating a culture that values continuous learning and improvement.

To maximize the efficiency and effectiveness of business software, customization and optimization are key. Tailoring the software to meet specific business needs and workflows allows for a more streamlined and efficient operation. The book highlights the importance of workflow optimization, which involves analyzing existing processes, identifying bottlenecks, and utilizing the software's capabilities to automate and improve those processes. Integrating the software with existing systems further enhances productivity and data consistency across the organization.

Security and data protection are paramount considerations in software management. With the increasing frequency and sophistication of cyber threats, businesses must implement robust security measures to safeguard sensitive data. The book emphasizes the need for encryption, access controls, and regular security audits to ensure data integrity and protect against unauthorized access. Additionally, compliance with privacy regulations is essential, and businesses must stay informed about evolving regulations and adjust their software management practices accordingly.

Ongoing software maintenance and upgrades are vital to ensure the long-term sustainability and relevance of business software. By establishing maintenance plans and performing regular updates and patches, businesses can address software vulnerabilities, introduce new features, and improve overall performance. The book emphasizes the need for evaluating the necessity of software upgrades and managing software licenses and support contracts effectively. These practices contribute to a seamless and uninterrupted software experience, enabling businesses to leverage the latest advancements in technology.

Successful software management also requires effective project management principles. By creating comprehensive project plans, defining milestones, and tracking progress, businesses can ensure that software initiatives are completed on time and within budget. The book emphasizes the importance of managing risks, engaging stakeholders, and fostering effective communication throughout the project lifecycle. Effective project management ensures transparency, collaboration, and the successful delivery of software projects.

Looking towards the future, the book explores emerging trends in the industry and their potential impact on business software. Technologies such as artificial intelligence, cloud computing, Internet of Things (IoT), and blockchain are transforming the software landscape. By staying informed about these trends, businesses can position themselves to take advantage of emerging opportunities and leverage these technologies to drive innovation and competitive advantage.

www.ingramcontent.com/pod-product-compliance
Lightning Source LLC
LaVergne TN
LVHW061527070526
838199LV00009B/408